PROMISED LAND

Penn's Holy Experiment,
The Walking Purchase,
and the Dispossession of Delawares,
1600–1763

Steven Craig Harper

Lehigh
University
Press

Bethlehem: Lehigh University Press

Associated University Presses
2010 Eastpark Boulevard
Cranbury, NJ 08512

The paper used in this publication meets the requirements of the American National Standard for Permanence of Paper for Printed Library Materials Z39.48-1984.

Library of Congress Cataloging-in-Publication Data

Harper, Steven Craig, 1970–
    Promised land : Penn's holy experiment, the Walking Purchase, and the dispossession of Delawares, 1600–1763 / Steven Craig Harper.
        p.   cm.
    Includes bibliographical references and index.
    ISBN 0-934223-77-7 (alk. paper)
    1. Pennsylvania—History—Colonial period, ca. 1600–1775.   2. Delaware Indians—Land tenure—Pennsylvania—History—17th century.   3. Delaware Indians—Land tenure—Pennsylvania—History—18th century.   4. Indian land transfers—Pennsylvania—History—17th century.   5. Indian land transfers—Pennsylvania—History—18th century.   6. Indians of North America—Pennsylvania—Government relations.   7. Pennsylvania—Ethnic relations. 8. Frontier and pioneer life—Pennsylvania.   I. Title.
    F152.H38   2006
    974.8′02—dc22   2005021547

for Jennifer Elizabeth

Contents

Acknowledgments

I GRATEFULLY ACKNOWLEDGE THE HELP OF SO MANY CONTRIBUTORS TO this manuscript. The late Lawrence Henry Gipson, a fellow Idahoan, provided the Gipson Fellowship that enabled me to do much of the research. Jean R. Soderlund shared her expertise on the Lenape and William Penn, read several drafts and returned penetrating comments and advice, endured all the flaws, and donated her editorial expertise. I acknowledge the kind assistance of Michael Baylor, Stephen Cutcliffe, Michael Raposa, and Roger Simon.

The accommodating Emma Lapsansky, Curator of the Quaker Collection at Haverford College, together with Joelle Bertolet, Elisabeth Potts Brown, and Diana Franzusoff Peterson, made my tenure there a delightful and rich research experience. The Historical Society of Pennsylvania was foremost among an array of repositories that have preserved and facilitated access to the documents that inform this history. Paul Peucker, Archivist of the Moravian Archives, generously facilitated my requests. Mark Turdo, Curator of the Moravian Historical Society, shared a wealth of relevant knowledge and resources. Tom Agostini engaged in encouraging discussions that enriched the book significantly. Richard Bushman and Terryl Givens furnished formative insights. Jane Merritt, William Pencak, and Daniel Richter all gave encouraging and useful criticism. Robert Kocsis extended Pennsylvania hospitality, acquainted me geographically, and gave me hope that, perhaps, there may be an interested lay readership. Alyssa Walker painstakingly transcribed much of the source material. Brent Roper created the most accurate and aesthetically pleasing map of the Walking Purchase ever made. Judi Mayer, Christine Retz, and Susan Thornton at Lehigh University Press served me with professional courtesy and efficiency. My department chairs and deans provided generous access to funds donated freely by many faithful anonymous supporters.

My parents remain a source of constant encouragement, support, and confidence; my siblings, too. My father helped me survey the Walking Purchase on the basis of available data, resulting in a more accurate sense of its bounds and dimensions than even the original surveyors could have accomplished with the technology available to them. Hannah, John, Abigail, Seth, and Thomas give this book proper proportions of momentousness and insignificance. Jennifer deserves my deepest gratitude. For her I am as Portia in Shakespeare's *Merchant of Venice*.

> Though for myself alone
> I would not be ambitious in my wish,
> To wish myself much better, yet, for you
> I would be trebled twenty times myself

PROMISED LAND

1

Introduction

THIS BOOK RECONSTRUCTS THE WORLD DELAWARES INHABITED FROM THE time Europeans arrived on their shores to their geographical and ethnic annihilation from the Delaware River valley in the 1760s. Focusing on the 1737 Walking Purchase as the central event in this declension narrative, the book observes the transformation of a fragile if generally peaceful middle ground, habitable by Delawares and English on negotiable terms, to an English colony determined to possess a boundless landscape by fraud and force.[1]

Just months after King Charles II promised William Penn a tract of land in America in 1681, Delawares met Penn's agents and exchanged "great promises . . . of kindness and good neighborhood, and that the Indians and the English must live in love, as long as the sun gave light."[2] The integrity of such promises depended on how "the Indians and the English" conceived of the landscape. To Penn it was all promised him by Charles II, but even more by a Supreme Being who expected Penn to build a new Israel characterized by peace and harmony. Even so, to Penn it was Penn's Woods, with emphasis on the possessive. Inhabitants of Lenapehoking were asked to relinquish their claims by signing deeds. Delawares, meanwhile, needed a benefactor, an ally to support their effort to maintain an existence independent of Iroquois domination. They entrusted that role to William Penn, whose agents arrived conveniently on this scene making desirable promises. Initially, then, Delawares and Penn incorporated each other into their political and ceremonial arrangements.[3] Beginning in 1682, Delawares negotiated with Penn and his agents in meetings marked by remarkable give and take. A 1682 deed between Delawares and Penn's agents describes the land to be deeded and includes the normal legal terms about "full and peaceable possession and seisen of the within granted tract and tracts of land." But it includes amendments that were probably appended to acknowledge Delaware power and persuade more Dela-

13

wares to accept the deed's terms.[4] One of the amendments to the 1682 document specifically codified peaceful coexistence between Penn's colonists and their predecessors on the landscape. By 1737, though, the deed drafted to confirm the Walking Purchase emphatically forbade, forever, Delaware presence.

The poles represented by these two deeds define the limits within which Delawares had power to negotiate both geographical and cultural boundaries once Charles II granted Penn's charter in 1681. Moreover, the contrasting deeds highlight Penn's internal ambiguity. His inheritance of English gentility, including its penchants for condescending colonialism and conspicuous consumption, militated against the mollifying influences of his Quakerism and gave Pennsylvania a bipolar legacy. Penn's sense of promised land was inseparable from a paternal notion of accountability to Providence for stewardship of the land's original inhabitants. Though Penn's altruism has been overstated by hagiographers and artists for a willing public, it existed as part of a precarious mixture with a thoroughly colonial mentality. When his heirs seized that self-interested strand of their father's ambiguous legacy they lost what informed any semblance of just, pacific, and equitable relations with Delawares. Politically weak and increasingly crowded by colonists, Delawares could no longer dictate the terms of geographical or cultural boundary disputes. Feeling the same pressures, the more powerful Iroquois joined the Pennsylvania government to force Delawares from the land. By the 1720s, Pennsylvania stopped incorporating and began resisting Delawares, who, in turn, fought to preserve their already circumscribed power in an increasingly possessive culture. The Walking Purchase of 1737 marked the end of negotiated boundaries in Pennsylvania, both geographical and cultural.[5] Dispossessed by the fraudulent purchase and the conspiratorial diplomacy before and after it, Delawares chose variations on several responses.

The first Delawares to host Penn and his agents negotiated with remarkable power. Decentralized political power actually worked in their favor, as Penn sought to maintain peace by negotiating with multiple Delaware kinship leaders who claimed rights to the Delaware River valley. In these meetings, Delawares gave little and received much, or so it appeared. Moreover, by 1684 Delawares forcefully arrested settlement north of Philadelphia over demands for more goods in return for accommodation. Penn capitulated in the face of Delaware power, but the episode revealed his willingness to possess Pennsylvania forcefully if necessary.

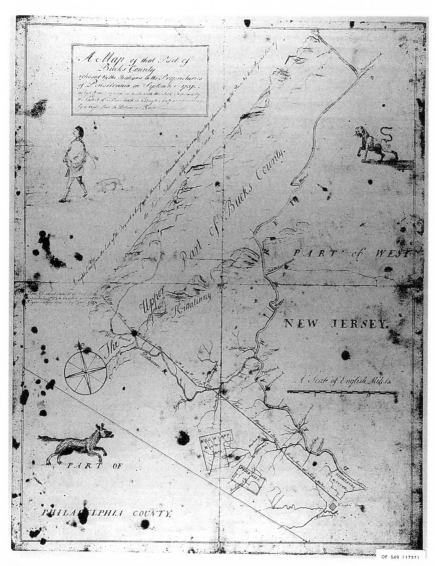

The Historical Society of Pennsylvania (HSP), Map of the Indian Walking Purchase (1737), Benjamin Eastburn. Pennsylvania Surveyor General Benjamin Eastburn's map of the Walking Purchase.

A generation later Nutimus and others negotiated and, failing
that, migrated. In the next generation Weshichagechive and his kin
adapted Moravian Christianity. Tishcohan (later known as Captain
John), negotiated in part by joining the Moravians. Tunda Tatamy
and his family became Presbyterians. Teedyuscung migrated,
adapted Moravian forms to his purposes, then struck violently back
before leading Delawares again into boundary negotiations in the
late 1750s. This time, however, only pretense was possible for the
Pennsylvania government. It had broken its promise to coexist. It
could no longer conceive of a landscape habitable on any other
terms than its own, and it had no incentive to imagine since it now
had sole power of possession.

2

Lenapehoking

They call themselves Lenni Lenape Indians or Woapanachke,
that is people living toward the rising sun.
—C. A. Weslager, *The Delaware Indians: A History*

BEFORE PENNSYLVANIA THERE WAS LENAPEHOKING, THE UNSURVEYED
greater Delaware River valley with its tributary streams and their sur-
roundings. No one knows for certain how long the Lenape had been
there or whence they came. Much of their history, even after European contact, remains "somewhat puzzling."[1] But mediators like the
Moravian missionaries who learned Lenape, combined with modern
ethnography and archaeology, reveal a substantial if often ambiguous picture of precontact Lenape history and culture. The first few
decades after European discovery of the Delaware Valley are clearer.
During this period the Lenape were called "Delawares" by Europeans after Virginians named Delaware Bay for Governor Sir Thomas
West, the third Lord de la Warr.[2]

   This naming complicates the matter of identifying the Lenape.
Anthropologist Marshall Becker maintains that the Lenape proper
composed only one of the many Native American groups in the
Delaware River valley. He argues that the "Jerseys" and "Munsees"
(also Minsis) were "distinct and separate" groups living, respec-
tively, across and up the river from the Lenape.[3] Writing in the late
eighteenth century, the Moravian cooper and ethnographer John
Heckewelder considered Lenape and Delaware interchangeable.
"Delawares who fixed their abode on the shores of the Atlantic divided themselves into three tribes," he wrote. Heckewelder learned
firsthand that the Lenape were the original people or ancestors of
these three and other distinct groups of Native Americans of the
northeastern woodlands.[4] So Heckewelder's use of *Lenape* meant the
original peoples of the Delaware Valley, including those covered by

17

the "Delaware" umbrella: the Unami of the Lower Delaware Valley (Becker's Lenape), the Unalachtigo of what is now New Jersey, and the Munsees, who gave the name *Minisink* to their territory in the Upper Delaware Valley. Ives Goddard largely followed Heckewelder. He added an important insight, however. Each of the Delaware sub-groups considered themselves unbound by the Delaware River. The southern valley Unami speakers, their northern neighbors the Una-lachtigo speakers, and the Munsees north of the Delaware Water Gap all spanned the river and inhabited the banks of its tributary streams east and west.[5] Including all three groups among the "Len-apes" or "Delawares" seems most consistent with the Lenape con-ception of themselves as the original people.

"The Delawares say," wrote the Moravian chronicler Loskiel, cit-ing early Moravian missionaries, "that the heavens are inhabited by men, and that the Indians descended from them to inhabit the earth: that a pregnant woman had been put away by her husband, and thrown down upon the earth, where she was delivered of twins, and thus by degrees the earth was peopled."[6] In 1679 an old Lenape man responded to the question of a Dutch colonist about the ori-gins of his people. The elder thought a few moments, took a piece of coal from the fire, and began to draw on the ground. "He first drew a circil, a little oval, to which he made four paws or feet, a head and a tail. 'This,' said he, 'is a tortoise, lying in the water around it,' and he moved his hand round the figure, continuing, 'This was or is all water, and so at first was the world or earth, when the tortoise gradually raised its round back up high, and the water ran off of it, and thus the earth became dry." A tree grew from this dry earth. From its root grew a man and from its bough a woman and from them the Lenape.[7]

This genesis story is notable not only for its account of Lenape origins but its reference to pictography. Zeisberger reported that the Lenape did not write "except the painting of hieroglyphics." They did, he said, make red pictographs to memorialize heroic deeds.[8] An observer of Delawares in 1775 noted that they passed along their history by "hieroglyphics and tradition."[9] In 1822 an eccentric natural history professor at Transylvania College, Con-stantine S. Rafinesque, reportedly inherited a pictographic Lenape history, the "Walum Olam," from a mysterious Dr. Ward, who re-ceived it for treating Delawares in Indiana. Rafinesque learned Len-ape from the dictionaries of Moravian missionaries and translated the "Walum Olam," which he published in 1836. Its strange provenance makes it suspicious as an authentic Delaware text, yet Rafinesque seems decidedly innocent in motive, if careless in documentation. Considered by most to be either fraudulent or, most likely, an effort of eighteenth-century nativists to revive traditional Lenape culture, the "Walum Olam" is possibly an ancient text.[10] Weslager admired its consistency with archaeological and ethnographic accounts.[11] He considered it reflective of a mythical tradition, embellished to be sure, but carrying at its core an essentially accurate, archaeologically supportable tale "of a movement of humans from west to east across the North American continent."[12]

Scholars generally have the Lenape originating somewhere in Asia and migrating in large numbers to northeastern North America during prehistory, following mastodons and mammoths.[13] When asked about their origins by Europeans in the midseventeenth century, the Lenape answered that they migrated from the west, alternatively by boat or by land. They considered themselves the original people.[14]

Ives Goddard estimated a Lenape population of eleven thousand in 1600.[15] More recently Becker (defining Lenape narrowly) relied on archaeological evidence to posit a total population that never exceeded five hundred.[16] Thomas Sugrue argued that Becker underestimated by failing to weigh European pathogens as determinants of Lenape depopulation.[17] The Florentine explorer Verazzano may have reached Delaware Bay as early as 1524, and surely the Lenape experienced European pathogens indirectly before they encountered Henry Hudson in 1609, but it remains unclear how dramatically Lenape demography was affected. Becker implies that a lack of archaeological evidence of pandemic deaths minimizes the mortality toll of European contact. European accounts, however, seem to suggest otherwise. A German, Reverend Daniel Pastorius, noted in 1694 that "many of these savages have died, even since I came here, so that there are hardly more than a fourth part of the number existing that were to be seen when I came to the country ten years ago."[18] Four years later a colonist reported 90-percent mortality.[19] "The Indians themselves say," reported Gabriel Thomas in 1698, "that two of them die to every one Christian that comes in here."[20] These are hardly scientific numbers and frustratingly late to reveal the impact of initial European contact with the Lenape. Clearly the Lenape, as other native groups, suffered demographic, economic, and cultural upheaval in the first decades after contact, but Becker posits a per-

suasive scenario suggesting that Lenape lifestyle at contact mini-
mized the early effects of European pathogens.

In 1600, Becker maintains, the Lenape lived in kinships no larger
than forty and foraged for their subsistence, leaving little for archae-
ologists to find. They were not primarily agricultural, he argues, citing a lack of evidence for corn storage. The Lenape grew but did
not store corn. They lived rather softly on the landscape in small
groups, roving to fish, hunt, gather, and grow in season for subsistence. Such social and economic organization kept the Lenape population relatively small compared to more sedentary, politically
centralized neighbors like the Iroquois.[21] Each kin group evidently
laid claim to a specified hunting and gathering territory. These
often overlapped and were regarded as "a medium of existence"
rather than a commodity.[22]

Whether these territories were alienable depends on intentions
and definitions. The Lenape were willing from early contact to mark
European land transfer documents that gave the Dutch, Swedes,
then English rights to specified lands. Lenape behavior, however,
shows that they intended by these documents to allow European access to land and its resources in exchange for desirable goods. To
suppose that they intended to alienate land in the European sense
projects on the Lenape an utterly foreign concept.[23]

Kinships were organized by matrilineage though with a male sachem who spoke in councils, treaties, and land negotiations. At
times loose confederations of kinships appear to have been under
the leadership of a grandfatherly sachem, but authorities agree on
the decentralized and democratic social, political, and economic organization of the Lenape. Sugrue wrote, "The contact-era Lenape
lacked the strong, cohesive tribal organization that enabled natives
in other parts of British North America to resist European encroachment."[24] It is true that the Lenape had no equivalent of the Iroquois
League, and that crippled their negotiating power in the eighteenth
century, but it does not follow that they failed to resist, even as they
accommodated, European encroachment.

3

Possession Lawfully Taken

This Country did belong to the crown of England, as well by
ancient discovery as likewise by possession lawfully taken.
—Thomas Young, "Relation of Thomas Young, 1634,"
in *Narratives of Early Pennsylvania*

FIFTEEN YEARS AFTER HENRY HUDSON DREW EUROPE'S ATTENTION TO
Delaware Bay in 1609, Dutch colonists working for the West India
Company encamped on Burlington Island before relocating to Manhattan. Willem Verhulst, provisional director of the West India Company in Delaware Bay, had orders to trade wares to the Lenape for
small parcels of land and secure written contracts saying so.[1] Two
land transfer documents from the Dutch colonization of Delaware
Bay survive. A June 1, 1629, deed conveyed a strip of land along the
west shore of the bay in what is now Delaware from ten Lenape men
to four Dutch patroons in exchange for "cloth, axes, adzes, and
beads."[2] Nearly two years later the same Lenape men conveyed to
the same patroons a larger tract across the bay. These transfers were
ambiguous. The documents marked by the Lenape assured all who
could read them that they "give up, abandon, and renounce" forever their claim to the land. The Lenape were doing something
quite different. They neither read the documents nor understood
the distinctly European legalese if interpreted to them.[3] They valued
trade goods—cloth, axes, and beads—for both practical and ceremonial uses.[4] It made good sense to accommodate the Dutch in
such an exchange. The possibility that a few patroons would encroach seemed remote.

In early 1631 the Dutch founded the whaling post Swanendael in
present Delaware on the land conveyed two years earlier. In 1632
the Lenape slew every last colonist. When West India Company officer David De Vries visited the bay in December he found it as empty
as Roanoke almost a half-century earlier. A Lenape man explained

to De Vries how the massacre occurred. The Dutch had performed
a ceremony of possession, in Patricia Seed's apt wording, by planting
a pole on which hung the emblem of the Seven United Provinces.[5]
When a Lenape sachem took material from the sign to use in making tobacco pipes, the Dutch became upset. De Vries reported:

> The Indians, not knowing how it was, went away and slew the chief who
> had done it, and brought a token of the dead to the house to those in
> command, who told him they wished they had not done it, that they
> should have brought him to them, as they wished to have forbidden him
> to do the like again. They then went away, and the friends of the mur-
> dered chiefs incited their friends—as they are a people like the Italians,
> who are very revengeful, to set about the work of vengeance.[6]

Clearly cultural and linguistic gulfs between Europeans and the Lenape remained long after the Atlantic crossing. Written agreements,
signed and remunerated, caused the Dutch to consider themselves
in possession of the boundless landscape, which they ceremonially
signified. The Lenape simply consented to Dutch presence and
gained desirable goods for doing so.

These differences of perception resulted in tragic miscommunications. When Lenape violated European ideas of property the extreme Dutch reaction made the offense seem a grave evil worthy of
death. When the Lenape learned after presenting their "token of
the dead" that the misdeed required only a verbal warning, their
extreme reaction cost the lives of everyone in Swanendael. It was not
the last time that culturally conditioned perceptions of land violently divided the Europeans and Lenapes. Swanendael proved only
the first chapter in the imperial story of Lenape trying to please Europeans for the advantages of trade at the cost of ecological and cultural upheaval and a reputation for being "very revengeful, to set
about the work of vengeance."[7]

Ironically the Delawares were decidedly nonaggressive except
when driven to extreme measures or intoxicated. With Hudson's discovery, news of the prodigious numbers of furs available drew West
India Company agents to bargain with Delawares, whose geographical position made them the envy of the Iroquois to their north and
the Minquas of the Susquehanna River valley. By the 1630s, hostile
Minquas drove Delawares to the east side of the Delaware River. The
Iroquois responded to sustained contact with Europeans, with its
mixed blessings of trade and demographic crises, by extending

control over subordinate groups via the mourning war system.[8] The Iroquois ceremonally feminized the Delawares to denote both pacificism and subordination. The swirling factors of growing dependence on European goods, increased harvesting of fur-bearing animals, and escalating hostility from Minquas and Iroquois encouraged the Lenape to accommodate the Dutch.[9] Meanwhile, according to Delaware tradition, their first portentous experiences with the West India Company included a fraudulent land negotiation and the introduction of alcohol.[10] The Delawares were swept into a vortex.

During the summer of 1634 the Delawares thought they found a truer patron. The English Captain Thomas Young, an adventurous London gentleman on a self-appointed search for the Northwest Passage, sailed into Delaware Bay and "tooke possession of the countrey, for his Ma[jestie], and there sett up his Ma[jestie's] armes upon a tree, which was performed with solemnities usuall in that kind." His men "fell a trucking" with Delawares, who sought his aid in warding off hostile Minquas. Young's men gave them trinkets in exchange for "Beaver and Ottor skinnes, which they would trucke with me for such commodities as I had." As Young made his way up the Delaware he met with numerous "kings," some "ancient" some "yonger," each of whom seemed to him "the proprietor of that part of the River, wherin I then rode." Young met the Delaware desires for protection and goods, treated them "lovingly" as a "Brother of their kings," and sent word back to England of the enormously profitable venture. "The people are for the most part very well proportioned," he wrote, "well featured, gentle, tractable, and docile. The land is very good and fruittfull and withall very healthful. The soyle is sandy and produceth divers sorts of fruites. . . . The Countrey is very well replenished, with deers and in some places store of Elkes. The low grounds of which there is great quantitie excellent for meadowes and full of Beaver and Otter."[11]

Except for a meddlesome Dutch presence, which, according to Young's narrative he gallantly overthrew, he found the valley full of "divers other things which with industrie will prove excellent good commodities," and he recommended that England plant colonists in this "most healthfull, fruitfull, and commodious River in all the North of America." Young described how he told Dutch traders "that this Country did belong to the crown of England, as well by ancient discovery as likewise by possession lawfully taken," and that he had been sent to "take possession." Too enamored with the illusive Northwest Passage to take up colonizing himself, Young spent only a few summer weeks in the river. Charles I was preoccupied, too. If they ever stopped, the Dutch resumed trading with Delawares as soon as Young sailed away.[12]

In 1638 Sweden asserted claim to the Delaware Valley and courted the Delawares for land concessions to legitimize claims the Dutch had assumed since Hudson's discovery. Peter Minuit, formerly employed by West India but now leading the New Sweden Company, showered the Lenape lavishly with trade goods in return for their marks on deeds that quit their claim to large tracts of land in the Lower Delaware Valley. In return Delawares furnished Minuit 1,769 beaver pelts and 314 otter besides the hides of "raccoons, sables, gray foxes, wildcats, lynxes."[13] For these Delawares expected continuing supplies of goods. Writing in 1759, the Reverend Israel Acrelius unintentionally captured the cultural miscommunications that marked seventeenth-century exchanges between Lenape and Swedes for land, furs, and manufactured goods: "It is true the savages sold their lands at a low rate, but they were a discontented people, who, at no great intervals, must have new gifts of encouragement, if their friendship was to remain firm. Such they always have been, and still are. As they regarded the Swedes and Hollanders as one people, it was all the same to them which of them had their land, provided only that they frequently got bribes."[14] What Acrelius thought payment for land the Delawares considered reciprocity for accommodation; what he thought bribes they supposed compensation for ongoing environmental encroachment. This misunderstanding persisted, plaguing relations between Delawares and Europeans in the years ahead.

While Swedes and Dutch competed for Delaware land and furs in the mid-seventeenth century, Delawares were positioned to take advantage of the competitive European trade. Not without its perils, this situation made Delawares vulnerable to the Minquas and Iroquois, to whom they became subject. The grandfather of Thomas Campanius Holm kept a journal of his experiences in America from 1643 to 1648, which informed Holm how Delawares were made "subject and tributary to" Minquas.[15] Attesting in 1697, Captain John Steelman wrote "that the Delaware Indians live at Minquannan about nine miles from the head of Elke river & fifteen miles from Christeen & thirty miles from Susquahanah river & are about three hundred red men & are tributary to the Senecars [Iroquois] and Susquahannahs [Minquas]."[16]

The seventeenth-century "orgy" of fur taking, as Weslager described it, depleted the Delaware watershed of beaver.[17] Quite suddenly, Delawares were no longer positioned to negotiate from power. They turned to corn as a cash crop for Swedish colonists. Otherwise they were but a nuisance to the Swedes, whose governor, Johan Printz, proposed to deal directly with the Minquas by dispatching the Delawares altogether.[18] "We have no beaver trade whatsoever with them," Printz wrote in 1644, and so proposed that "nothing would be better than to send over here a couple of hundred soldiers" to wrench "the necks of all of them in this River." Then, Printz continued, "we could take possession of the places (which are the most fruitful) that the savages now possess" and outstrip European competitors by directly trading with Minquas fur suppliers.[19]

As Delawares lost Swedish goods to Minquas in the European trade, they too began to think of violent alternatives. "The Indians murmured that they did not receive more, and that the Swedes had no more goods for their traffic. Then there came out a rumor that the savages had a mind to fall upon and exterminate them." Only mature minds among the Delawares, if Acrelius's account is reliable, prevented a Swedish Swanendael.[20] The same fate, presumably, grounded Printz's proposal to exterminate the Delawares.

In 1655 the West India Company regained control of the Delaware River valley from the New Sweden Company, but Dutch dominance was again short lived. With the Stuart Restoration to the throne in 1660, English interest in the Delaware Valley revived. Charles II granted the valley to his brother, James, duke of York. Four years later the Dutch at New Amstel on Delaware Bay surrendered to a tiny English armada. Under English governors, Delawares continued to cede land to Europeans by marking documents and receiving desirable goods. The relationships among Delawares, Minquas, and Iroquois during the middle decades of the seventeenth century remain clouded, but certainly a complicated choreography of power seeking and taking transpired.[21] Spanish, French, English, Dutch, and Swedish colonists courted Native Americans, the latter three empires in the seventeenth-century Delaware Valley. Meanwhile Minquas, Iroquois, and Delawares sought working relationships with the various empires of Europe. Francis Jennings noted that Delawares "had a neat profit from the cycle" of European trade, but it did not last, and Delawares did not remain in a position of power, though they sought desperately to retain profitable, protective relationships. Some of what Jennings viewed as evidence of Delaware independence is better understood as loosely organized efforts to forge alliances for fear of hostile neighbors and loss of trade, a familiar scenario in colonial diplomacy and one that emerges clearly from early sources like Thomas Young's narrative of his summer on the river.[22]

When Delaware Valley furs were gone and European colonists able to grow their own corn, Delawares were situated tenuously and undoubtedly felt pressure from the Minquas first and then, when they retreated to Maryland, the Iroquois directly. Whether some conquest occurred that escaped documentation in the scraps of available evidence or, more likely, a less militaristic but nonetheless potent process of subordination took place, Delawares recognized by the early eighteenth century that the Iroquois had made them subordinates.[23] The Delaware sachem Sassoonan conceded in 1712 that the Iroquois "had subdued them."[24]

Delawares responded to such shifting balances of power creatively, not complacently, with both English colonists and Iroquois. Even so, given their small numbers and decentralization, Delaware responses were limited. If they escaped some of the demographic devastation of European pathogens, they had no mourning war culture to replace what significant losses did occur. Nor were they politically organized to negotiate a balancing of European powers. With few exceptions, Delawares were routinely regarded lightly by European governors, whether Printz or later the benevolent but Iroquois-minded Sir Edmond Andros. In such a condition, Delawares were bound to become dependent upon or subordinate to some stronger power. By the eighteenth century that power was the Iroquois. But a long history of diplomacy, trade, and land transfer with Dutch, Swedes, and English made Delawares savvy to the idea of playing a European benefactor against the Iroquois. The problem, the Delawares recognized, was "when the English come they drive them from their lands."[25] By the 1670s Delawares had to face the hard reality that they were "surrounded by Christians" on whom they were dependent.[26] What they needed was a legitimate benefactor, one committed to the idea of peaceable possession, willing to deal kindly, promote trade, and pay for lands while allowing Delawares continued access to the landscape and its ecosystems.

When Charles II granted William Penn "all that tract or part of land in America" on which Delawares lived in 1681, they had unknowingly gained an ally, a Brother Onas, as they came to know him, determined actually to act out the cliché of the other European colonizers. Penn's sincerity is evident in his first communiqué to the Delawares. He wrote:

> I am very sensible of the unkindness and injustice that has been too much exercised towards you by the people of these parts of the world, who have sought themselves, and to make great advantages by you, rather than be examples of justice and goodness unto you; which I hear has been matter of trouble to you and caused great grudgings and animosities, sometimes to the shedding of blood, which has made the great God angry. But I am not such a man, as is well known in my own country. I have great love and regard toward you, and I desire to win and gain your love and friendship by a kind, just, and peaceable life.[27]

Whether Penn's ideals, described as "peaceable possession," a pairing of words fraught with tensions, could be sustained or even realized in America remained to be seen. And Penn's holy experiment yielded anything but a holy city for Delawares to inhabit, yet because he thought it would, the watershed of Penn's gaining possession of Pennsylvania marked an improvement in European colonization.

4

Peaceable Possession

The English and they [Delawares] live very peaceably, by reason
the English satisfies them for their Land.
> —Gabriel Thomas, "The History of West New Jersey,"
> in *Narratives of Early Pennsylvania*

THE SPIRITUALITY THAT INFORMED WILLIAM PENN'S SINCERE AND ARTICU-
late ideals of tolerance, justice, and humanity clashed with potent,
culturally conditioned aspirations that often countered his theology.
This conception of Penn, hardly novel, is best and most recently ar-
ticulated by Richard Dunn.[1] Still, this Penn has never been con-
nected to the Walking Purchase of 1737, by which Penn's heirs
defrauded and dispossessed the descendants of Delawares with
whom their father negotiated mutually satisfying relationships. The
indelible but ambiguous moral legacy Penn bequeathed to Pennsylvania gave his heirs two clear precedents to inform their relationships with Delawares. They chose the well-worn road.

William Penn was as remarkably unique a person as he was a man
of his time and place. As son and namesake of Admiral Sir William
Penn, brilliant young William aspired to gentility and familiarity at
the courts of Charles II and later James II. He also became rapt in
the apocalyptic theology of George Fox and contributed his own
corpus to the powerful current of radical religiosity called Quakerism. One of Fox's themes was the "new found World" destined to
be planted by "God's English Israel." Ideally situated to bridge otherwise impassable social, cultural, and geographical worlds, Penn
acted out Fox's vision.[2] He could, as William Comfort wrote, "take
a step that no other Quaker could have taken: he had the opportunity to found beyond the seas an asylum for those in England and
Europe who were oppressed for conscience's sake."[3]

Having petitioned for American land in lieu of debts owed his
father, on March 4, 1681, Penn received from Charles II a charter to

28

Pennsylvania with liberal though limited rights to settle and govern as he saw fit.[4] Mary Geiter thought Charles II granted Pennsylvania as part of a calculated strategy to pacify his opponents in the restoration crisis. "He sought to avert the possibility of civil war by dividing his opponents, appealing to moderate elements among them. . . . The launching of Pennsylvania conformed with the opposition ideology that religious toleration and limited monarchy were more conducive to commercial expansion than 'popery and arbitrary power,'" and thus satisfied London merchants eager for expanded trade with a new American colony. Geiter considers this interpretation to preclude the possibility that Pennsylvania came of Penn's "desire for a religious utopia." Only an artificial dichotomy, however, limits the ability to conceive of Penn's ideals as mixing liberally with the peculiar political situation, resulting in a remarkably liberal charter's being granted to a Quaker creditor.[5] Penn's remarkably prescient ideals of toleration rendered his plans for Pennsylvania not merely an outpost of tolerance for dissenters, but an example for all the world—a New Jerusalem.[6] Whatever political maneuvers Charles II may have made in granting Pennsylvania, Penn was sure that God was finally behind it.

This Providence came of the Supreme Being's desire to establish "an example" of toleration in the context of English monarchical government to show a bitterly divided nation that peace could obtain if kindness, justice, and forbearance were safeguarded. In August 1681, Penn wrote to James Harrison, a Quaker minister in northern England's Bolton, Lancashire, of his successful petition. Penn had relied on "the Lord in the obtaining of it," and wanted Harrison to know he gave credit where it was due. Moreover, Penn desired to be worthy of God's providence to him by using his plantation for holy purposes, "that an example may be set up to the nations." Before outlining the particulars, Penn momentarily waxed idyllic about the American woods. "There may be room there, though not here, for such a holy experiment."[7] The secularization of Penn's "holy experiment" has come to signify an experiment in civil government. Penn meant something closer to what current English renders as "holy experience."[8]

Penn's 1681 correspondence shows how he envisioned Pennsylvania as analogous with the Hebrew Mount Zion or the Christian New Jerusalem, that is, as a holy city, not simply a political experiment. Penn's frame of government and civil liberties were adaptable means to the holy end he envisioned. Since that end never material-

ized and no longer resonates with most Americans, secularization
of the holy experiment celebrates Penn's methods and forgets his
anticipated end. For Penn himself, however, the whole reason to
"observe and reprove mischiefs in government" and ensure liberty
of conscience was his conviction that God had impressed him to pre-
pare a place for "His people."[9]

Penn's August 25, 1681, letters to James Harrison and Robert
Turner allude to Old Testament passages in which promised land is
designated for the chosen people for the purpose of erecting "an
example, a standard may be Sett up to the Nations."[10] To Quaker
minister Thomas Janney, Penn wrote of Quakers' being "heirs to the
promises" of Israel's patriarchs—including promised land—and testified that he never had more powerful spiritual urging than he felt
in his quest to obtain a charter to Pennsylvania.[11] That Charles II
granted Pennsylvania despite opposition was Penn's evidence of
providential favor. So Penn wrote that he was "firme in my faith that
the L[or]d will prosper it, if I & they that are & may be ingaged, do
not greeve him by an unworthy use of it." Then Penn seamlessly
shifted to particulars about land, commissioners of property, quit-
rents, acreages, and deeds. He wrote of the need for "blessed gov-
ermt, & a vertuous ingenious & industrious society, so as people may
Live well & have more time to serve the Ld, than in this Crowded
land. God will plan Americha & it shall have its day: or Gloryous day
of Christ in us Reserved to the last dayes, may have the last parte
of the world, the setting of the son or western world to shine in."[12]
Anticipating the last days, end of the world, and setting of the Sun,
Penn was pleased that God had given him a western world in which
to plant the holy city. Penn named it Philadelphia, the city most
closely associated with New Jerusalem in the Revelation of St. John.[13]
In 1684 Penn prayed for his holy experiment, embodied in Philadelphia, with a plea that she would "stand in the day of trial" and be
"preserved to the end."[14] This vision of the world informed William
Penn's celebrated relations with Native Americans.

Shortly after receiving his charter in 1681, William Penn instructed agents to meet with Delaware Indians living on the west side
of the Delaware River and "soften them to me and the people, let
them know that you are come to sit down lovingly among them. Let
my letter and conditions with my purchasers about just dealing with
them be read in their tongue, that they may see we have their good
in our eye, equal with our own interest." Then Penn wanted presents given to the Delawares as gestures of his goodwill and evidence

of "a friendship and league with them according to those conditions." The letter to which Penn referred informed the Delaware of
the "one great God and power that hath made the world and all
things therein, to whom you and I and all people owe their being
and well-being, and to whom you and I must one day give an account
for all that we do in this world. This great God hath written His law
in our hearts, by which we are taught and commanded to love and
help and do good to one another, and not to do harm and mischief
one to another."

Penn further explained how the God to whom he referred, in
league with the king of England, had given him the land on which
the Delawares lived, and he expressed his "desire to enjoy it with
your love and consent, that we may always live together as neighbors
and friends." Acknowledging that other Europeans had abused Delawares, Penn assured them he and his people wanted to win their
confidence with kindness, justice, and peace. Penn then told the
Delawares that before he arrived he would be sending agents to treat
on his behalf and to enter a "league of peace."[15]

On April 10, 1681, Penn commissioned his able cousin, William
Markham, to proceed to Pennsylvania as deputy governor "to Survey
Sett out, rent, or Sell lands."[16] Six months later, on October 25, he
appointed William Crispin, William Haige, John Bezar, and Nathaniel Allen as commissioners of property. When Crispin, a cousin of
Penn, died en route, Thomas Holme was appointed to fill his
place.[17] Markham and the commissioners went to Pennsylvania with
instructions to establish amicable relations with the Delawares that
would lead to trade, land purchases, and "peaceable possession."[18]
To accommodate the transfiguration of Pennsylvania from an amor-
phous concept to an increasingly specified place, Penn developed
an organizational structure that historians have conglomerately
called the Land Office.[19] Besides commissioners of property, he appointed a proprietary secretary; a surveyor general with deputies in
each county; a master of the rolls to record deeds, leases, and mortgage records; and a receiver general to manage his local accounts.
Frequently men such as William Markham, Thomas Holme, and
later James Logan served simultaneously as a commissioner and in
one or more of the other roles. After 1685, Markham served simultaneously as the proprietary secretary, secretary of the provincial council, and, after 1687, commissioner of land.[20]

In April 1682, Markham negotiated with Delaware "Indian
sachemakers" for land bounded by a line beginning at a white oak

tree on the west bank of the Delaware River and running west to Neshaminy Creek "and along by the said Neshaminy Creek unto the river Delaware. . . . And so bounded by the said main river to the said first-mentioned white oak in John Wood's land."[21] On July 15, 1682, twelve Delaware leaders "acknowledg themselves fully satisfied, contented, and paid" by receipt of

> three hundred and fifty fathoms of wampum, twenty white blankets, twenty fathoms of stroudwaters, sixty fathoms of duffels, twenty kettles (four whereof large), twenty guns, twenty coats, forty shirts, forty pair of stockings, forty hoes, forty axes, two barrels of powder, two hundred bars of lead, two hundred knives, two hundred small glasses, twelve pair of shoes, forty copper boxes, forty tobacco tongs, two small barrels of pipes, forty pairs of scissors, forty fishhooks, two handfuls of needles, forty pounds of shot, ten bundles of beads, ten small saws, twelve drawing knives, four ankers of tobacco, two ankers of rum, two ankers of cider, two ankers of beer, and three hundred guilders.[22]

Convinced they had negotiated advantageously, the sachems marked a legal document giving "William Penn, his heirs and assigns, forever. . . . full and peaceable possession and seisen of the within granted tract and tracts of land." A few weeks later six more sachems came forward with claims to the purchased land, and, for ten guns, marked the deed "as valid, effectual, and sufficient for the conveyance of the whole lands and others within named to the said William Penn, his heirs and assigns, forevermore, as if we had then with the other sachemakers signed and sealed the same."[23]

Dutch and Swedish colonization dating from 1632 gave Delawares experience with European ways. Moreover, Penn gained knowledge of Delaware ways as a proprietor of West Jersey. Still they could only comprehend each other through the refracting lenses of their own assumptions. Penn warned his agents to prevent controversy by only buying land "of them where any justly pretend, for they will sell one another's if you be not careful."[24] Indeed, four of the sachems who signed the July 15, 1682, deed had formerly sold some of the same land to New York governor Sir Edmond Andros in 1675.[25]

These negotiations reveal important assumptions held by both involved parties. The twelve sachems who marked the July 15, 1682, deed did so knowing that other sachems had simultaneous claim to the same land. And those sachems who got ten more guns from Penn by adding their marks to the deed considered themselves justified and wise. For land was a fluid, shared substance to the sparsely settled Delawares, while kettles, hoes, axes, scissors, guns, woolen blankets, fishhooks, and rum were highly coveted. The Delawares were eager to deal with William Penn, and he was usually pleased that for a substantial investment in manufactured goods he could promote trade, purchase land, and preserve peace.[26]

The July 15, 1682, deed gave Penn "full and peaceable possession" of the land. Those were precisely his goals. In Penn's world land could be possessed; one could own it and send surveyors to impose arbitrary lines upon it. According to Patricia Seed, neither Dutch, French, nor Spanish colonists considered private property, with its surveyed boundaries, quite as crucial to legitimate possession of the New World as the English.[27] Penn's Englishness made him think of land as a commodity. It could be sold to buyers who would subdue and improve it by building fences and planting gardens. And it promised to yield handsome returns as waves of settlers poured in from Europe and the population naturally increased in the American woods. By contrast, Delawares described the land by referring to the usefulness of its various ecosystems.

The observant Pennsylvania surveyor, Lewis Evans, wrote in 1755 that the original inhabitants of Penn's woods "do not generally bound their Countries by Lines, but by considerable Extents of Land. For as their Numbers are not considerable in Proportion of the Lands they possess, they fix their Towns commonly on the Edges of great Rivers for the Sake of the rich Lawns to sow their Corn in. The intermediate Ground they reserve for their Hunting, which equally serves for that Purpose and a Frontier."[28] Delawares thought in terms of summer residences, hunting areas, berrying places, trails, and fisheries. Colonists relied on these features as markers that made subdivided sense of an otherwise contiguous landscape. The 1682 deed invites its readers to envision boundaries by referring to "a certaine white oak," "gray stones over against the Falls of Dellaware River," and a "white oak marked with the letter P standing by the Indyan Path."[29] It calls on natural features—a river, a white oak—to facilitate its readers' visualization of a boundless landscape in terms of the subjective geometry to which they were accustomed. Most tellingly, it assigns the subdivisions to individuals, as in "John Wood's land."[30] Pennsylvania colonists were legally and psychologically conditioned to possess the land by survey and subdivision. Before they could use it they needed to "subdue" it by fencing, plowing, planting, and grazing domesticated animals. Generally the

English thought, too, that because indigenous peoples failed to subdue the land after the English fashion, their claims were void.[31]

Here, however, William Penn parted company with more typical
English thinking. "Possession," for English purposes, was essential,
but in Quaker Pennsylvania possession was best preceded by "peaceable" purchases like the 1682 transaction. Fortunately for Penn, Delaware conceptions of land and desire for advantageous alliances
initially accommodated the peaceful coexistence he sought. As the
1682 deed shows, workable agreements could be made to share natural resources. An amendment to the deed codified such an alliance
and ensured everyone continued access to the landscape and its ecosystems. It says that Penn's agents "may freely pass Throug any of
Their lands as well that wch is not purchased as that wch is with out
molestio[n] as They doe quietly amongst us."[32] Nevertheless, Penn's
assumption that Delawares could "sell one another's" land reflected
myopic acculturation by a world with private possession of alienable
land.[33]

Though Evans understood well, as Penn did, that Delawares used
the landscape as their "larder," he assumed they had more land
than needed since their "numbers are not considerable in Proportion of the Lands they possess." The "intermediate ground" to
which Evans referred appeared to Penn to be woods in need of subduing by survey in anticipation of sale. For Delawares it served as
shared space that sustained life both biologically and culturally. As
Delawares and colonists acted on these assumptions, Delawares
began to feel threatened as soon as colonists began fencing their
"frontiers," long before colonist occupation of actual village sites.
The English had arrived to render Pennsylvania woodless as quickly
as possible. Delawares "could not imagine, and did not want, a
world without woods."[34]

Beginning in 1681 Penn marketed his tract on terms that compro-
mised Delaware conceptions of space. He promoted Pennsylvania
with this promise of land: "The shares I sell shall be certain as to
number of acres; that is to say, every one shall contain five thousand
acres, free from any *Indian* encumbrance, the price £100."[35] Delawares began to resent the encroachment caused by such acreages
before they recognized they were cumbering land they had alien-
ated by accepting desirable goods and marking papers. Delawares
and Penn shared needs and hopes for cooperation. Even so, the idyllic relations for which Penn hoped, and for which he is renowned in
the folk history of Pennsylvania, were threatened when the proprie-

tary desire for land on which to settle colonists competed directly with Delaware territoriality.

At these times English property ways conflicted with Delaware ways. By February 1684, Tammany, the legendary Delaware sachem, "played the rogue," according to Surveyor General Thomas Holme, by "hindring our peopl to plant & seat upon their lands by war!" By threatening to burn the homes of newcomers, Tammany effectively arrested settlement of and thus revenue from Bucks County land.[36] The problem, from Tammany's perspective, came of Pennsylvania's failure to offer Delawares regular gifts as reciprocity for accommodation. Tammany complained that he was owed "nine guns, eight Duffull match coats, ten blankets . . . in consideration of the gift of land" between Pennypack and Neshaminy Creeks, which he had deeded to William Penn in 1683. Provincial councilors tabled consideration of Tammany's "request" until William Markham could be consulted. They hoped, meanwhile, to pacify Tammany with "two gallons of rum."

Misunderstanding Tammany's ideas of property, William Penn responded as an English parent would: "You must make them keep their word," he told Holme, "and if the Indians will not punish him, we will and must." Penn wrote in the voice of an English proprietor, not a pacifist, to hold "Tamine" accountable before the law, since he had "sould all" the land in question and was therefore acting "Rogueish."[37] Tammany begged to differ, and William Markham knew it. Markham reported in August 1686 that all the Delaware sachems with claims on Bucks County land "threatened to kill Israel Taylor if he surveyed any more land before it be bought." Markham tried to meet this demand.[38] Tammany and the other Delawares backed down as Bucks County settlement abated. Probably softening occurred in both Tammany's demands and Penn's paternalism, owing to the need each had for the other. Tammany forced Penn's acknowledgment of Delaware hospitality. For Penn, forcing Tammany to be neighborly undermined the purpose of Pennsylvania. These early clashes revealed the distinct property ways of the English Quaker and the Delawares. Their peaceful resolution revealed the mitigating tendencies of Penn's idealism and Delaware desires for English goods and alliance. Most importantly, Delawares exercised significant control over land usage early in Penn's holy experiment. Delawares negotiated on their terms well into the 1680s. James O'Neil Spady observed that "after Penn's founding of Pennsylvania, compromise was increasingly a Lenape obligation, and brotherhood and friendship increasingly required Lenape subordination."[39] That is clear from this historical distance, but the Delawares who signed Penn's deeds, including Tammany, felt less impotent and regarded the situation as more nuanced and less determined. Penn's government, after all, began supplying Tammany with regular gifts, made plans to purchase the land in question, and meanwhile stopped sending settlers to occupy it prematurely. Tammany, in turn, stopped acting "rogueish." Delawares compelled Penn to establish his famous policy, "neither to take possession himself nor suffer others to possess themselves of any lands without first purchasing them from the Indians who had a right to them."[40]

The conflict between Tammany and Penn hinted at the economic tensions that plagued Penn's idealism. Grieving over his mother's death and concerned for his wife's health, Penn delayed his voyage to Pennsylvania. Then, just a week before he finally sailed in August 1682, Penn learned that his finances, entrusted to his Quaker steward Philip Ford, were out of order. Ford received the income from Pennsylvania land sales as well as Penn's English and Irish properties. He used this revenue to meet Penn's everyday obligations as well as negotiate the charter and advertise the new colony. He also sent goods worth nearly three thousand pounds to Pennsylvania on Penn's behalf. Penn learned suddenly from Ford that administering Pennsylvania was costing rather than compensating him, and that Ford had personally floated £2,851 to cover expenses. Understandably concerned that land sales in Pennsylvania could dwindle, and that he might never see Penn again once the proprietor embarked for the colony, Ford drafted documents that bound Penn to a mortgage for 300,000 acres of Pennsylvania and a six-thousand-pound security bond for the outstanding debt. Shipboard and anxious to see America, Penn signed his trusted steward's documents uncritically. As the implications of this arrangement became clearer to him, though, Penn reviewed his accounts carefully and accused Ford of impropriety. Even so, Penn's dispute concerned only a fraction of what he owed Ford, which grew under compound interest. Finally Penn "first mortgaged, then leased, then sold Pennsylvania to Ford" in 1696, when Penn continued to oversee the colony as rentier and steward, paying Ford for the privilege. When Ford died in 1702 he bequeathed his right to Pennsylvania to his heirs, who, in Richard Dunn's wry description, sued Penn "in the courts of Exchequer, Common Pleas, and Chancery to recover debts, damages, and Pennsylvania."[41] When he lost the suit in Common Pleas, Penn went to debtor prison in 1708. He raised £7,600 to settle his dispute with Ford's heirs and so escaped further litigation.[42]

Meanwhile, though, before the weight of these matters pressed him so, Penn embarked for America aboard the *Welcome* in late August 1682, apparently unaware that the documents just signed would haunt him. He endured a voyage in which smallpox slew thirty-one of his fellow passengers and wrote to Ford that six weeks after losing sight of England they "saw it in America; and being about twelve leagues off from the coast, the air smelled as sweet as a garden new blown." Penn's garden simile situated him in the English tradition of considering the New World an English garden to be planted, cultivated, and therefore possessed.[43] "Men may say," he wrote in 1683, that "our wilderness flourishes as a garden," suggesting that possession, though peaceable, was possession nonetheless, and on English terms.[44]

The day after his arrival Penn met with Dutch and Swedish settlers, the first Europeans to plant in the Delaware River valley, as well as more recently arrived English, "assuring them of their spiritual and temporal rights: liberty of conscience and civil freedoms. All he prayed, expected, or required, was sobriety and loving neighborhood." An old Swedish captain felt his soul stirred.[45] Penn next sought to solidify peaceful relations with Delawares. This is when the legendary Great Treaty is reputed to have taken place with Tammany at Shackamaxon. It is most likely lore grown out of several meetings between Penn and Delawares in which goods and promises were exchanged and genuinely amicable relations established. In a 1683 letter to a group of English investors, Penn wrote, "I have had occasion to be in council with them upon treaties for land, and to adjust the terms of trade." He went on at some length about Delaware customs in these meetings, presenting an observant report remarkable for what it reveals about Delaware ways and Penn's own assumptions and anxieties.[46]

Penn noticed the importance of consultation, order, and oratory in these meetings and became convinced that Delawares were not fools. Their experience with Dutch and Swedish traders served them well. Penn reported a speech in which a Delaware orator "fell to the bounds of the land they had agreed to dispose of, and the price (which now is little and dear, that which would have bought twenty miles not buying now two)." Penn continued admiringly, "They do speak little, but fervently, and with elegance. I have never seen more natural sagacity, considering them without the help (I was going to say, the spoil) of tradition; and he will deserve the name of wise that outwits them in any treaty about a thing they understand." He noted, too, that "when the purchase was agreed, great promises past between us of kindness and good neighborhood, and that the Indians and the English must live in love, as long as the sun gave light."[47] Though the historicity of a single great treaty under the legendary elm at Shackamaxon cannot be certified, Penn's willingness to negotiate, stemming from obedience to Quaker principles of peace and the humanism implied by the inner light, is well established.

Penn's report to the Free Society of Traders is remarkable for another reason, too—namely, for the way observing Delawares caused Penn to reflect on English culture. Penn observed not only that Delawares neglected to hoard goods but that their kings voluntarily subdivided acquisitions and seemed remarkably content with "little." Penn made these observations of Delawares in contrast to the English:

> In liberality they excell, nothing is too good for their friend; they give them a fine Gun, Coat, or other things, it may pass twenty hands, before it sticks; light of Heart, strong Affections, but soon spent; the most merry Creatures that live, Feast and Dance perpetually; they never have much, nor want much: Wealth circulateth like the Blood, all parts partake; and though none shall want what another hath, yet exact Observers of Property. Some Kings have sold, others presented me with several parcels of Land; the Pay of Presents I made them, were not hoarded by the particular Owners, but the neighbouring Kings and their Clans being present when the Goods were brought out, the Parties chiefly concerned consulted, what and to whom they should give them? To every King then, by the hands of a Person for that work appointed, is a proportion sent, so sorted and folded, and with that Gravity, that is admirable. Then that King sub-divideth it in like manner among his Dependants, they hardly leaving themselves an Equal share with one of their Subjects: and be it on such occasions, at Festivals, or at their common Meals, the Kings distribute, and to themselves last. They care for little, because they want but little; and the Reason is, a little contents them: In this they are sufficiently revenged on us; if they are ignorant of our Pleasures, they are also free from our Pains. They are not disquieted with Bills of Lading and Exchange, not perplexed with Chancery-Suits and Exchequer Reckonings.[48]

One imagines that Penn's observations of the Delawares and the occasion of writing this letter may have stirred ruminations over his financial arrears. It was obvious that the natives "have not had their passions raised to the same degree of luxury of Europe," but neither, Penn noted, "have they the anxieties that follow those pleasures."[49]

Pennsylvania Quaker folklore maintains that during one of these meetings, Penn and the Delawares, probably including Tammany, reached an agreement for land lying west of the Delaware River and north of the July 15, 1682, purchase. They concluded that Penn and Delaware representatives would walk north together for three days and impose a boundary at the end of their walk to run east to the river. Penn would then buy the enclosed area for an agreeable amount of goods. As the story goes, after a day and a half Penn was satisfied that more than enough land had been covered and an agreement was reached to walk the remaining day and a half at an unspecified future time.[50]

The Delawares had their own versions, which told that "about the Time of the great Fresh at Delaware Falls," William Penn "talk'd of purchasing of the Indians" a tract of land "up the River as far as a Spruce tree . . . & farther a Day & a half's Walk wou'd extend." On an unknown date, "one James Yeates a tall Man living with W. Penn & some Whitemen & Indians" started at the spruce tree and walked up the Delaware "to the Mouth of Thoiccon & thence up the same to that Branch thereof which stretches over the nearest to Cosshohoppen." After going "a small Distance," at noon the next day they stopped "and mark'd three large White Oaks on the West Side of the Creek." The western boundary of the proposed purchase ran from the three oaks to the "South Sun till it fell in with the line" of the 1682 purchase. The Delaware tradition said that after this walk "Penn went to England, but without making the Indians any Pay for the Lands which they expected at his Return."[51] Another account, shared by natives and settlers alike, had William Penn agreeing with Unami Delawares "for as much Land as a man could walk out in a Day & half." William (rather than James) Yeates and another man

> were appointed to walk it & two Indians were to attend them. The walkers were to lead a Horse & to stop and sit down when they eat Dinner, & the Indians were to have time to Smoke a Pipe before they started, they were to proceed from a Spruce Tree, the Boundary of former Purchase, & follow the Course of ye River till they came to Tohicon Creek & then follow the Course of said Creek till they finished the Journey.[52]

In 1759, Penn's son Thomas reported the version of the story he favored, that the walkers went well beyond Tohickon, and "when the Men were got as far as the West Branch they differed about which Branch they should go up," the Delaware or the Lechay (or Lehigh as it is now known).[53] Delawares believed that the conflict rose from more than an innocuous if puzzling fork in the river. When the walkers insisted on going north beyond Tohickon Creek, Delawares objected strenuously: "The Indians refus'd, telling them they had not recd. Orders from their Nation to travel up the Creek, & that their Rights extended no farther up the River for that the Land beyond sd Creek belonged to the Unalimi or upRiver Indians. Here they disagreed and returned home without finishing the Walk. William Penn soon after return'd to England & the Matter remained unsettled."[54] According to another account, "the Dispute grew so high that the travellers proceeded no farther." Further negotiations were scheduled, but "in the mean time Wm. Penn went to England & afterwards died," as did the Delaware sachem. The walk was never satisfactorily executed, nor the land ever paid for.[55]

It remains unclear whether this initial walking purchase occurred between 1682 and August 1684 while Penn was in Pennsylvania or after he left for England, or, less likely, during his second sojourn in Pennsylvania from 1699 to 1701. The only documentation of it other than the imperfect reminiscences cited are an incomplete 1686 deed and an extract from a letter Surveyor General Thomas Holme sent to William Penn, suggesting that the unfinished paperwork was drafted August 25, 1686, after Penn's departure. Significantly, no original deed has ever been found. Even with chronological uncertainty, the consistency of Delaware accounts is compelling evidence that the negotiations finally came to nothing, an outcome both Delawares and Pennsylvania officials assumed until 1736.

The episode remains shrouded because the Penn heirs and James Logan decided in 1736 to assert the validity of the incomplete 1686 document they described as a copy of an August 25, 1686, deed. Historians have too willingly trusted them.[56] There is no proof that a 1686 purchase was concluded.

The closest thing to such evidence is Holme's August 25, 1686, report to William Penn, in which he noted, "I gave thee account of my transactions with the Bucks Indians about the purchase there; it was long and chargeable, but could not be avoyded. I wrote to P[hillip] F[ord] to send the things for them against next spring, being then to pay them off."[57] From this it appears that the August 25,

1686, purchase was valid, but there is more to Holme's report, which hints at the more likely scenario, consistent with Delaware accounts, that the transaction was never finalized since the goods agreed upon were not forthcoming. Holme continued, "Till all is paid, we can have no lines run; nor have we a penny raised on pub[lic] account to defray of any pub[lic] concernes." Holme went on to express his frustration that Pennsylvania settlers were unwilling to foot the bill.[58] Though specific details are elusive, given the state of Penn's accounts, he could do little to alleviate the situation. Pennsylvania settlers, Holme vented, were able but unwilling to pay the Delawares. Penn was willing but unable. The next year, 1687, Penn replaced his commissioners of property and gave the new appointees fresh instructions. When agents of Penn's heirs tried in the 1750s and 1760s to convince Sir William Johnson that the 1686 transaction had been finalized, they presented only extracts from several letters, none of which proves their case. Rather, phrases like "when the Indians are paid" reappear conspicuously in 1687 and 1688. An extract from a William Markham letter says that Delawares received some of what was owed them on April 21, 1688. The Penns' agents presented evidence of intention but could not demonstrate conclusive consummation of the 1686 walking purchase.[59] As Delaware tradition put it, "the Matter remained unsettled." When the purchase was revisited in August 1737, Delawares were hesitant. They were willing to grant that their ancestors relinquished rights to the land south of Tohickon Creek, but they had no memory of ceding any land north of that bound.[60]

Penn returned to Pennsylvania only once more, and for less than two years, but he brought the influential James Logan with him in 1699.[61] Logan was a gifted and scientific man, more interested in Newton's *Principia* than George Fox's Quakerism. He was genteel and learned, shrewd and diplomatic. Though a Quaker, Logan forsook the peace testimony for a more pragmatic posture of favoring expedient defense of Pennsylvania. Penn recruited him to fill Markham's role and gave Logan instructions to collect in one place all the records relating to proprietorial land affairs.[62] In a succession of appointments, Logan was made receiver general, a commissioner of property, member of the Provincial Council, and provincial secretary. Though the constellation of titles would change somewhat over the years, Logan remained provincial secretary until, after masterminding the Walking Purchase, he retired to Stenton, his estate north of Philadelphia in 1736, at which time an Anglican, Reverend

Richard Peters, replaced him.[63] Considering the length of his tenure and the authority vested in him, no other single person, including Penn himself, was positioned to influence Pennsylvania land policy more than James Logan.[64] During Penn's brief second stay in Pennsylvania, he negotiated with Delawares for land along the Delaware River between Neshaminy and Tohickon Creeks.[65]

Logan kept abreast of this and other land negotiations. In fact, before and after Penn recovered the unfettered proprietorship of Pennsylvania in 1708, land policy was largely the domain of James Logan. By his May 27, 1712, will, Penn conveyed the colony upon his death to his second wife, Hannah Callowhill, and her six children. The will made Hannah sole executrix, who, advised by appointed trustees, was to steer the affairs of the colony until her male heirs—John, Thomas, and Richard—came of age. A series of strokes in the following months largely incapacitated William Penn, leaving Pennsylvania business more than ever in the hands of the Assembly, the Provincial Council, and the Provincial Secretary James Logan. When Penn died in 1718 Logan and the other commissioners of property assumed control of the colonial holdings on behalf of the mortgage trustees. The Land Office went into a holding pattern. Though the tide of immigration increased considerably during these years, patents were granted infrequently, apparently only often enough to pay Penn's mortgage.[66] When Hannah Penn died in 1725, the commissioners of property administered the estate for the Penn heirs.

On Logan's watch, Pennsylvania cleared land lying along the Delaware River northeast of Philadelphia of Delaware Indian claims. In 1718, according to the Presbyterian schoolmaster Charles Thomson, who served as a clerk in treaty negotiations before becoming the secretary of the Continental Congress, an "enquiry was made into Land Affairs by the Proprietary Commissioners and the Delaware Indian Chiefs; that the old Deeds were carefully inspected, the Bounds of the Purchases made of the Indians at sundry Times fully ascertained." To forestall future difficulties, Delawares granted a "Deed of Confirmation" that released claim to "all the Lands they had heretofore sold the Proprietaries, namely from Duck Creek to the Lechay Hills which are southward of the Forks of Delaware."[67] Sassoonan was the spokesman of Delawares situated west of Neshaminy Creek. He and five others acknowledged that Penn compensated them for land between the Delaware and Susquehanna rivers and south of the Lehigh River valley. The sachems accepted guns, coats, kettles, and blankets as a gift in memory of the recently deceased Quaker proprietor, upon receipt of which they granted

> release and forever Quit-claim unto the said William Penn his heirs & Assigns all the Said Lands situate between the said two Rivers of Delaware and Sasquehanna from Duck Creek to the mountains on this side Lechay and all our Estate Right Title Interest property Claim and Demand whatsoever in and to the same or any Part thereof so that neither we nor any of us nor any Person or persons in the Behalf of any of us shall or may hereafter lay any claim to any of the said lands or in any wise Molest the said William Penn his Heirs or assigns or any Person claiming by from or under them in the peaceable & quiet enjoyment of the same.[68]

Meanwhile a band of Delawares led by Nutimus began to occupy a village above the northern line of the 1682 purchase but south of the hills that set off the Lehigh Valley.

In 1682, William Markham needed to satisfy different Delawares who laid claim to the proposed purchase. Similarly, James Logan needed to satisfy Nutimus before Pennsylvania could lay unencumbered claim to Delaware Valley land north of the 1682 purchase. In 1726, Logan privately purchased some of this land from Nutimus with plans for constructing an iron production facility. Pennsylvania law forbade private Pennsylvanians from buying land from Native Americans, but who was to prevent James Logan from doing so? Delawares were willing so long as the alliances did not encroach territorially and continued to pay dividends. Logan kept this peace but piecemeal removed Delaware claims to Delaware Valley lands, laying a legal groundwork for dispossession with the kind of agreeable purchases William Penn preferred. Moreover, Logan continued to make Penn's mortgage payments until Pennsylvania became, in 1730, the sole proprietary of John, Thomas, and Richard Penn, to whom their mother had allotted the province. In the meantime, however, Logan occasionally warranted Delaware Valley land to himself and a few others, knowing he had no pretense to do so.[69] In 1702 Logan bought five hundred acres of land in what is now Solebury Township. He and the other commissioners sold 5,000 acres above Tohickon Creek to John Streiper in 1701, 580 acres to William Beeks in 1702, and 2,500 to John White a year later.[70] With the Penn heirs back in command of the province, Logan lost ultimate control of land affairs and became an agent in the accelerated process of dispossessing Delawares based on William Penn's policy of peaceful possession of the land.

At least one William Penn hagiographer cast Penn's indebtedness in the best possible light. Catherine Peare painted the Ford family as insolent, deceitful usurers who put a principled and resolute Penn in debtor prison "for conscience's sake."[71] But Richard Dunn's assessment of Penn as a profligate spender as early as the 1670s implies that the proprietor's conscience, at least in regard to thrift, was applicable to others but not himself. As Dunn observed, just before Penn embarked for America in 1682, he directed his wife, Gulielma, to "cast up thy income and see what it daily amounts to by wch thou may'st be sure to have it in thy sight and power to keep within compass, and I beseech thee to live low and sparingly, till my debts are paid."[72] Penn wrote to James Logan in 1704, "If my son prove very expensive I cannot bear it, but must place to his account what he spends above moderation, while I lie loaded with debt and interest." Of the younger William's wife the patriarch was even more critical. "I wish she had brought more wisdom, since she brought so little money, to help the family," he wrote in 1707, using her spare dowry as an outlet for his anxiety and frustration over his own poor judgment and narrow options in the midst of the Ford estate litigation.[73] "Certainly," Dunn wrote, "Penn's greatest character defect, before and after the founding of Pennsylvania, was his inability to live within his means."[74] That defect transferred to his sons. They did not, however, inherit the Quaker consciousness that bridled Penn's appetites and prevented him from being a complete "voluptuary."[75] As they came into control of Pennsylvania in the face of mounting indebtedness and a rising tide of immigrants, self-interest would not be hampered by a Quaker conscience. For the Delawares, that translated into dispossession.

Delaware land was promised to William Penn by Charles II. Delawares were willing to have Penn plant and give them useful goods, so they exchanged good faith promises with Penn upon the land. The mutually agreeable relations that followed were possible because Delaware conceptions of the landscape facilitated shared access and Delawares needed powerful allies in their struggle to maintain independence from their aggressive northern neighbors of the Iroquois League. Penn considered the land to have been promised ultimately by God and "would not abase his love nor act unworthy of his Providence & So defile what came to me clean." Otherwise Pennsylvania could only be like other English colonies and therefore no "example," no "standard to the nations."[76] As long as Penn took his inspiration for Pennsylvania from the books of Daniel and the Revelation—as long as the "last dayes" were imminent in Pennsylvania—the Walking Purchase could be postponed. But William Penn's idealized vision of Pennsylvania died with him, if not before. He bequeathed only a condescending colonial mentality and debt. Anything holy about the experiment ended. The need to be peaceable no longer burdened English possession.

5

What Ye Indians Call Ye Hurry Walk

He will deserve the name of wise that outwits them in any treaty
about a thing they understand.
                    —William Penn to the Free Society of Traders, 1683

They accordingly had the Land walked over by what ye Indians
call ye hurry walk & instead of following the Course of the River
as they ought, they had a Line laid out by the Compass by wch:
they were enabled to travel over a Vast Extent of Country, & by
this time People came fast to settle the Land in the Forks, so that
in a short time it was full of Settlement & the Indians were
oblig'd to remove farther back.
                    —Account of the Walking Purchase by Moses Tetemie

UNLIKE THE EARLIER COLONIZED VIRGINIA OR NEW ENGLAND, PENNSYL-
vania avoided ethnic violence as it dispossessed its native inhabitants, at least until 1755. War was anathema in this pacifistic colony,
yet potent European weapons were brought to bear with devastating
consequence. Cartographer Mark Monmonier wrote, "The authority of maps in boundary litigation is long-standing and deep rooted:
maps so closely entwined with Western civilization's concept of
real estate that the owning, selling, and buying of land would be impossible without them. More than signatures and deeds, surveys and
property maps make real estate a reality."[1] In the 1730s the Pennsylvania proprietors and their agents employed the European weapons
of deeds, surveys, and maps to defraud and then dispossess Delawares. Pennsylvania's brand of peaceable possession accomplished
its aims less violently but no less potently, for as Jean Soderlund observed, the consequences of European colonization for Delawares
were no less severe than for Natives of New England, Virginia, or the
Carolinas.[2] Indeed, as Neal Salisbury explained, "the consequences
of the fraud were of utmost significance: the Delawares were removed."[3]

46

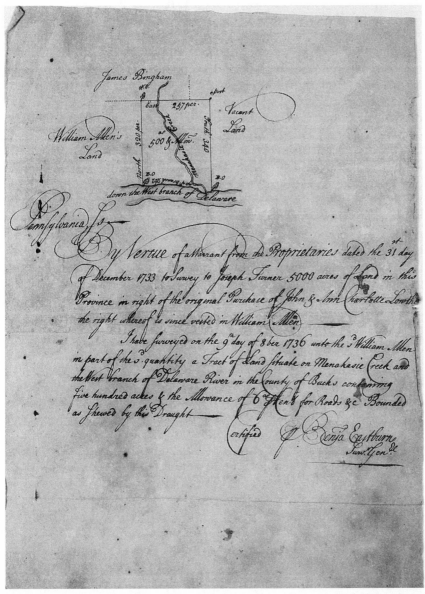

Moravian Archives, Bethlehem, Pennsylvania. Survey of 500-acre tract of land at the confluence of the Monocacy Creek and the Lehigh River (in present-day Bethlehem, Pennsylvania) for William Allen, October 9, 1736. Map of a 1736 survey by Pennsylvania Surveyor General Benjamin Eastburn based on a land warrant issued in 1733. One of many surveys conducted on Delaware lands before the Penns obtained permission. The process of dispossession of Delawares for possession by Pennsylvanians is shown by the terms "vacant land" and "William Allen's land," or "James Bingham."

The Penns and their agents brought the entire arsenal to bear in the mid-1730s. An old, unconfirmed deed became authoritative, secret surveys were conducted, and an illusory map drafted to transform Lenapehoking into Pennsylvania. As the Delaware interpreter Tunda Tatamy testified, the authority vested in these documents of dispossession persuaded Pennsylvanians that they could legitimately occupy Delaware lands.[4] Moreover, this pacifistic dispossession left no dissonance for future Pennsylvanians since the powerful weapons of dispossession seemed innocuous and civilized. It was possible for one Pennsylvania historian to write, "There is no doubt the Indians honestly believed they had been betrayed, but the facts lead us to believe that there was no intention on the part of the whites to demand only what *their deed* called for."[5] That deed was a document of betrayal, and its execution reveals the intent to defraud. But traditional explanations make Pennsylvania officials appear much less aggressive and duplicitous than they were. Those officials created an undying legend of their innocence, founded on the overstated benevolence of William Penn. Thus, when Delawares finally fought back in the 1750s, the violence could only be attributed to a recently developed notion of their "savagery."[6]

John, Thomas, and Richard, sons of William's second wife, Hannah Callowhill, gained control of Pennsylvania in 1730. Thomas, the businessman of the trio, moved from England to the province in 1732. John and Richard remained in England. Within two years they wrote to Thomas that their debts had reached seven thousand pounds, then eight thousand pounds. They were under an "absolute necessity" of receiving revenue generated in Pennsylvania. "We are very sorry," they wrote to Thomas, "we are obliged to write to you in this Manner but as Necessity has no law and we are under the Greatest you must excuse us, for to have nothing to Live upon but what Comes from thence and to be Continually dun'd for Debts that are due is Certainly the most uneasy Life a Person Can live under."[7] The only alternative John and Richard could see was to cut losses by selling the colony to the highest bidder since, as they wrote Thomas in May 1734, "we are now at the Mercy of our Creditors without anything to Maintain us."[8]

This pressure was the primary catalyst for what historian Francis Jennings characterized as "the gradual alteration in the postures originally taken by John and Thomas Penn and James Logan."[9] The Penns' agent in charge of the Land Office, James Logan, traveled to Pennsylvania with their father in 1699 and had been the single most influential official in the Land Office since. Formally a Quaker but free of the theological strictures that justified the holy experiment, Logan actively participated in the age of Enlightenment.[10] He was unfailingly loyal to the proprietary family and also had personal interests in Delaware Valley real estate.

The correspondence between Logan and William Penn's sons, together with land documents, shows that, despite assertions to the contrary, they knowingly abandoned a policy of removing encumbrances for patented lands by obtaining clear title from Delawares before selling the land to settlers. At a 1728 meeting with Sassoonan, who complained that "Christians settle on lands that the Indians have never been paid for," James Logan assured the aging Delaware sachem that William Penn "made it a rule, never to suffer any lands to be settled by his people, till they were first purchased of the Indians; that his commissioners had followed the same rule."[11] Logan betrayed the patent falsehood of this and similar statements in an earlier letter to the Penn heirs. Reporting a surveying foray into the Forks, Logan wrote in December 1727 that "the Indians would suffer no manner of survey to be made there on any account whatsover. There never was any pretense of a purchase made on thy Father's account within thirty miles of the nearest of these Indian settlements."[12]

As noted previously, Logan was personally invested in this land. Besides securing other acreages, he became part owner of the Durham Iron Works, located on a four-square-mile tract purchased from the Delaware sachem Nutimus in 1726. This land was "over Tohicon," or north, "beyond ye Bounds" of the 1682 purchase. Knowing this, Logan and his partners "sent for Nutimus Tyshikunk & some other Indians [and] purchased of them a tract . . . and thereby obtained their Consent to make that Settlement."[13] "Soon after" the Durham purchase, "Mr. William Allen took up land at Minisink," the area north of the Delaware Water Gap, which he purchased from the Penn heirs, leaving to them the obligation to pay the Delawares. Allen, in turn, sold some land to a French Huguenot named Nicholas Dupui.[14] Recognizing the potential havoc such transactions could wreak on Pennsylvania's successful Indian policy, James Logan urged the proprietors in 1728 to sell only land that was "clear of Indian and other Claims."[15] Logan knew that Pennsylvania never legitimately cleared land north of Tohickon Creek of all Delaware claims, not before 1728 and never thereafter.

The primary motive behind Thomas Penn's land sales was to generate revenue for the proprietors. Allen's interest was speculative. An elite Philadelphian of Scots-Irish ancestry, Allen was reputed to be the wealthiest man in Pennsylvania. He invested in land that he knew, on the basis of inside information, would shortly be free of Delaware claims. Value would then skyrocket and Allen would add to his fortune. There appears also to have been an effort on Logan's part, on behalf of the proprietors, to prevent Palatine immigrants settled in New York from crossing the Delaware and settling the Minisink. When some of these Germans "actually paid the Indians above twenty pounds per hundred" acres, Logan recognized the ominous precedent of free competition for land and reminded them in certain terms of Pennsylvania's proprietorial charter. He began imploring one or more of the Penn heirs to travel to Pennsylvania to feel the weight of these problems at close range and negotiate personally with the Delawares.[16] Meanwhile he sent Pennsylvania surveyors into the area and began earnestly exploring ways to acquire clear title to the Lehigh River valley.[17]

A Delaware hunting territory lay south of the Water Gap at the confluence of the Lehigh and Delaware rivers—the Forks. Before Thomas Penn could see his way clear to sail to Pennsylvania, the Penns sold twenty thousand more acres, location unspecified, to William Allen in 1729. Allen, Logan, and the Penns knew that the unspecified acres lay in the Forks of the Delaware. Logan urged John Chapman, the Bucks County deputy surveyor sent to measure Allen's tracts, to "take the utmost Care herein that no offense be given to any of the Indians."[18] Logan's correspondence during this period reveals his cautious nervousness. He occupied the unenviable position of facilitating the transition from William Penn's policy of purchasing Indian quitclaims before surveying and settling, to the Penn heirs' policy of selling land out from under the Delawares. Logan, Allen, and the Penns knew in 1729 that they were actively selling land to which they had no quitclaim from Delaware inhabitants. They knew there had been no terms reached or "considerations" paid for proprietary purchase of Forks land. Logan's letters reveal the uncomfortable culpability he felt in forsaking the policy of William Penn. He reminded the Penns that land "on Delaware above Tohickon Creek must be purchased," showing that at the time of his writing in 1728 the land had not yet been, and that he did not relish the responsibility of upsetting the established order.[19] The Penns sensed the tenuous situation, too, and replied, "We see the Absolute Necessity of Hastining the purchases with the Indians."[20] But for the

Penn heirs the dissonance generated by the prospect of upsetting Delawares an ocean away paled when compared to being "Continually dun'd for Debts that are due."[21]

Motivated by the welcome relief of William Allen's money, the Penn heirs sold thousands of acres in the Forks and Minisink before obtaining clear title. In the process they perceived or feigned continuity with their father's policy. Indebtedness, demographic growth, and the threat that the Penns might lose power to generate revenue via the province because of inability to regulate settlement demanded the change. Psychologically the shift was easier for Penn's heirs than for Penn himself because his sons were liberated from their father's vision for Pennsylvania. They did not intend their proprietorship to be a holy experience. They cared little whether Pennsylvania served the English world as a model society. Whereas William Penn was mindful of Delaware claims and remarkably inattentive to his debts, his sons were preoccupied with their accounts and less concerned with Delaware claims. Conditioned to gentility and prestige, embarrassed by their father's term in debtor prison, Penn's heirs could see no other way of protecting their proprietorship, not to mention their reputation. They persuaded themselves, "there is an absolute Necessity . . . to Raise all the Money that is Possible if we have any thought of Continuing the Whole Interest or appearing with any Credit in the World."[22]

In 1734 John Penn fled England and the dunning of creditors for Pennsylvania, arriving September 21. He had an idea, which he soon shared with Thomas. With land abundant and money scarce, why not turn the former into the latter in a more direct fashion than they were trying? Why not put a hold on issuing warrants and offer one hundred thousand acres to be divided among prospective settlers who purchased a forty-shilling ticket? Squatters who purchased could legalize their title to land. Others could pick out a spot "any where within the province, except on manors, lands already surveyed, or agreed for with the proprietors or their agents, or that have actually been settled or improved before the date of these proposals."[23] If successful, the lottery might have raised fifteen thousand pounds, but there were complicating factors, including a law against lotteries enacted by Quaker assemblymen who were sure to object on moral grounds in spite of John Penn's rationale that not even "the Most Godly can gainsay it" since "there is no fraud in it."[24]

Another complication came of the fact that the Penns technically owned but did not control or have practical claim to most Pennsylvania land. Whatever Penn's 1681 charter said about longitude and latitude, the fact remained that Native American claims limited the Penns' practical control of the province to the southeastern corner of the present state. Francis Jennings explained their dilemma. "From their constricted estate the Penn's only appreciable income came from the purchase money laid down for large tracts of land, and the only open spaces large enough to locate large tracts in were over the Indian line."[25] Since 1727 the Penns had been avoiding this problem by selling lands still claimed by Delawares. With John's arrival, that ill-advised policy continued with increased zeal. Still, the sold acreages were unprofitable to their buyers until Delaware quitclaims were obtained, since resale waited until colonists became confident that their purchases would not be cumbered by Delawares.

In October 1734 the Penns sought Logan's advice on inducing the Delawares to sell the Forks and inquired about proper prices if they should. Logan assured the proprietors, "You should purchase" and noted that two pounds per thousand acres seemed reasonable, but told the Penns that setting a price prior to a meeting would be "to no purpose" since they would be dealing with "the sharpest fellows to deal with that I have known amongst the Indians."[26] Logan knew whereof he spoke. He had dealt directly with Nutimus, the Delaware sachem at the Forks who sold the Durham tract to Logan. Thomas and John Penn sent word to Nutimus to ask him to go to Durham to treat with them. He did and the two parties met as their ancestors had, with at least a pretense that they could arrive at mutually agreeable solutions.

Existing records reveal no suggestion by the proprietors that they or William Penn had already purchased the land or considered the Forks their domain. Rather, even as the Penns sold Forks land to speculators, they acted as if the Delawares had legitimate claim on the land. The Delawares, for their part, willingly entertained offers. Both parties desired what the other could give, but the proprietors were under the greater pressure and therefore negotiated from weakness. Thomas Penn "kept begging and plagueing" Nutimus and the other Delaware leaders "to Give him some Land and never gives us leave to treat upon any thing till he Wearies us Out of Our Lives."[27] Nutimus recognized his position of power and held out for higher stakes. It was "as if they had an Inclination to be paid," the appalled lieutenant governor George Thomas later wrote of the Delawares.[28] The Durham meeting ended without any agreement, except another meeting planned for May 5, 1735, at the proprietary manor of Pennsbury.[29]

In the meantime Thomas and John Penn prepared. They knew they would not have means to pay Nutimus's price before the May meeting, so they gathered intelligence and devised a new strategy. Through research or perhaps sheer creativity, the unfinished transaction of 1686 came to the proprietor's attention. Tammany, then a Delaware sachem, had negotiated with William Penn's agents for land north of the 1682 purchase, as far as a man could walk in a day and a half, between the Delaware River and Neshaminy Creek extended north. No doubt mindful of this provision, Thomas and John Penn personally visited the Forks in late 1734 or early 1735 and found the "place very proper to build a town upon" because "the situation with regard to the river is certainly very advantageous."[30] It was most likely upon returning from their fact finding mission that the Penns ordered Timothy Smith, Bucks County sheriff, to oversee a party of walkers to determine how far hearty men could reasonably get in a day and a half. Early in the morning of April 22, 1735, the sheriff and deputy surveyor John Chapman set out on horseback from Chapman's Wrightstown farm. They were accompanied by footmen Edward Marshall, a twenty-two-year-old apprentice surveyor; James Yeates, a farmer from nearby Tinicum; and Joseph Doane of Wrightstown. James Steel, the proprietors' receiver general, wrote to Sheriff Smith on April 25 to inquire about the results of the trip. "The Proprietaries are impatient to know what progress is made in travelling of the land that is to be settled in the ensuing treaty that is to be held with the Indians at Pennsbury on the fifth day of the next month, and therefore desire thee, without delay, to send down an account of what has been done in that affair."[31]

When Steel heard nothing by April 29 he wrote again. The Pennsbury meeting was fast approaching and the proprietors were anxious for intelligence. They requested "that a messenger may be sent to give them account, without delay, how far that day and a half traveling will reach up the country."[32] The documentary record does not reveal when or how the Penns received a report of the trial walk, but they likely heard from Smith and/or Chapman and possibly Joseph Doane days or perhaps hours before the Pennsbury meeting. If so, they learned that woodsmen potentially could, with a path properly cleared, walk northwestward from Wrightstown, cross Tohickon Creek, and cover well over forty miles in twelve hours. Motivated walkers could reach the Blue Mountains south of the Lehigh River

in a day and cross the river and follow it through the Kittatinny
Mountains by the next midday.[33] That was precisely what the proprietors desired to hear. They now knew that the Forks—including the
surveyed tracts of Allen and other investors waiting only for Delaware quitclaims before they could be turned into cash—was within
the reach of a day and a half's walk. All that remained was the formi-
dable task of persuading the Delaware inhabitants to sign the land
away.

To that end the proprietors chose a strategy of employing historical records, with the intention of shifting power from the unlettered
Delawares back to them and the authority of their written records.
Between the October 1734 meeting at Durham and the May 1735
Pennsbury meeting, the proprietors recalled the useful 1686 negotiations. They were distant enough to be only vaguely remembered
and therefore subject to manipulation to fit current proprietorial
aims. The best documentation they could find was "an unconsum-
mated *draft*" of the 1686 transaction, which, if it was agreed upon,
would have given the proprietors claim to land north of the 1682
purchase as far as a man could walk in a day and a half.[34] This 1686
walking purchase was aborted. The document produced at Pennsbury purported to be a copy of the original. It outlined preliminary
terms for a land transfer but had glaring gaps regarding the direction and distance of the bounds of the tract in question. It bore no
signatures, signs, or seals. Very unlike other such documents, it
made no mention of payments made or due.

This weak document was evoked as authoritative only in despera-
tion. It was conspicuously absent from the October 1734 Durham
meeting. Nevertheless, if Delaware sachems refused to sell the land
to him, Thomas Penn could employ James Logan to argue that their
ancestors had sold it to Penn's father, an assertion the proprietors
had not made a few months earlier. They decided to act at Pennsbury as if the 1686 document, which proved nothing more than that
preliminary plans had been drawn, was proof that an agreement for
a walking purchase had been signed, sealed, and paid for.

At Pennsbury James Logan showed the Delaware sachems the
copy of the 1686 document and "made a Speech to the said Indians" designed to conflate the historical deed draft with a fictitious,
fully agreed upon and paid for transaction.

Among other Things, he mentioned to them the Purchase made from
their Ancestors of the Lands in and near the Forks of the River Delaware

by the Said William Penn Esquire or his Agents in the said Year 1686; and that the Purchase had been fairly made by the said old Proprietor for a large Consideration paid to the Ancestors of the said Indians, and a good Deed executed by them for the said Lands. That the Indians had always found and knew the old Proprietor to be an honest good Man, and that he allways was kind to and used them well, and never would permit any Lands to be settled till he had purchased and fully satisfied the Indians for them and that his sons the then Proprietors were therefore not a little surprized and concerned that they should now (as he understood some of them did) make Objections to or entertain any Doubts about that Purchase.[35]

Logan cleverly evoked William Penn's reputation and policy, mentioned specifically and thereafter implied that payment had obviously already been made, then summoned guilt by lamenting that the sachems "used to be esteemed an honest people."[36] Then, to provide the sachems "full Satisfaction respecting the Regularity and Fairness of the said Purchase," James Logan presented "Joseph Wood (who was an Anabaptist Minister) and William Biles Esquire," a longtime justice of the peace and former speaker of the Pennsylvania assembly, who swore to the Indians that they "were present in the year 1686 and saw the Said Purchase fairly made, and Part of the Goods mentioned in the Deed for it delivered to the Indians, and that he the said Joseph Wood was a subscribing witness to the said Deed." This testimony was both persuasive and problematic. Two witnesses, "both well known to the said Indians," had solemnly sworn. Still, they swore to witnessing the transfer of "Part of the Goods mentioned in the Deed," though one glaring feature of the copy is the absence of any mention of goods to be transferred.[37] Wood swore to having signed, yet no original deed with his signature, or any other, could be produced.

Tunda Tatamy, the Delaware interpreter, was at Pennsbury and left a detailed account of the deliberations, which focused not on the authenticity of the 1686 document, but on its interpretation. How far up the river did the Penns want land, and who, precisely, had the power to give it to them?

Thomas Penn insisted that the day & a half's Walk was to be made up the River & that Makeelikisko the Chief of the Unami's owned all the Land on the River Delaware. This Nutimus denied & said that the Land below Tohicon belongd to the Unami Indians & that they never claimed

a Right to any Land over that Creek, but that over Tohicon and upwards
belonged to the Unalimi or up River Indians of which he was Chief.

The debate endured for a week, with Nutimus insisting that the
Delawares who negotiated the 1686 agreement "did not intend to
convey to ye Proprietor the Lands above Tohicon because they knew
it was not their Right."[38] This was plain, Nutimus argued, from the
terms of the 1686 agreement, which specified, according to Delaware recollection, that the walk was to begin at the spruce tree on
the riverbank that marked the northeast corner of the 1682 purchase, and "proceed no farther up the Delaware than Tohicon," but
rather "up the River to the Mouth of Thoiccon."[39] It was then to
follow "the Course of that Creek" westward, and thus its northern
bound would fall far south of the Lehigh River valley.

Finding the sachem's knowledge of the 1686 transaction to be better than he anticipated, Logan "asked Nutimus how he came to
know what the Bargain was" as he must have been too young to witness the negotiations and the Delawares had no written records.
"Nutimus said he had it from his fathers. Besides from the Indian
way of selling Land he could not but know."[40] Nutimus then lec-
tured Logan on the Delaware way: "No Land can be sold without all
the Indians round being made acquainted with the Matter," because
"the Chief always—with the Leave of the others—undertook to
sell & when he had agreed he called together the head of the fami-
lies who had any Right in the Land sold & divided among them the
Goods he got for the Land." He explained the transaction:

> Then the heads of families again divide their portion among the Young
> people of their Family & inform them of the sale & thus every individual
> who have any right must be fully acquainted with the matter. Besides
> whenever a sale is made the Chief who sells calls the Chief of the neigh-
> boring Tribes who are his friends and have no right, in order to be wit-
> nesses of the Sale & to make them remember it he gives them a share of
> the Goods.[41]

Having failed to manipulate Nutimus, Logan tried to impugn his
claim by asking how he had any rights to land in the Forks since "he
was born in Jersey. Nutimus said his mother came from this side the
River, & by her he had a Right here." Tatamy remembered that
"Nutimus thought this a trifling question," and turned it on Logan
by asking "how he came to have a Right here as he was not born in
this Country?"[42] Nutimus further explained that the Delawares did

not conceive of the river as a boundary in the same way the colonists did. This exchange typified the different assumptions that informed English and Delaware property ways. Logan thought in terms of imposed boundaries and the absolute right of the English to the land. Nutimus thought of the land as fluid and exposed Logan's illogical premises.

Annoyed and increasingly desperate, Logan pressured Nutimus, telling him how bad it would be for his people if he failed to come to terms. A brilliant man used to power, Logan was unaccustomed to meeting his intellectual match. He blamed Nutimus for the deterioration of their relations. He assured the sachem and perhaps himself of his own power with outstretched arms, claiming that he was a "big man" while Nutimus, by contrast, was "as the little Finger of his left hand."[43] Logan had come to Pennsbury hoping that Delawares "would not raise any Disputes about that Purchase," but Nutimus did not recall that the 1686 agreement had ever been finalized and he would not relinquish the Forks.

From Logan's perspective the Pennsbury meeting with "Nootamis and his Associates" left the Delaware sachems "baffled" and "disappointed" to learn that their claims to the Forks, so recently acknowledged by the proprietors, were no longer. The Penns and James Logan rationalized their strategy to acquire the land by charging that Nutimus had all along just "pretended that a relation of his on this Side of Delaware left him his lands by will and Accordingly he came over and Claimed a great Quantity of Land to which the other had no right and made himself very troublesome." But there was, for Logan's purposes, no pretext when the proprietors "produced a Deed with witnesses yet living who had been ye rightful owners of that Land and had long before sold it" to the Penns.[44]

Some of the sachems went away from Pennsbury with ambivalent views. Tishecunk apparently thought that Logan was speaking straight, but Nutimus would promise nothing without first consulting elders to inquire more about the events of 1686, and as "Monawkyhiccon their Chief was then absent, they could at that time do nothing about it."[45] Such a dilatory denouement wearied the Penns and James Logan, who had used his best rhetoric to placate, then manipulate, then intimidate the Delaware sachems. Nutimus, who would have none of it, gave as well as he received.

Disappointed, the Penns in frustration gambled that the lottery might solve their troubles. On July 12, 1735 they initiated the lottery in language that specifically did not forbid settlement on lands cumbered by Delaware claims, but rather "any where within the province, except on manors, lands already surveyed, or agreed for with the proprietors or their agents, or that have actually been settled or improved before the date of these proposals."[46] Some of the patents issued based on lottery tickets were for land "situate on or near the West Branch of the River Delaware in the County of Bucks Metes and Bounds therein Particularly Specifyed," or in the "Fork of Delaware" or "situate on Menakasee [Monocacy] Creek which Falls into the said West Branch of the River Delaware." Some of these handsome tracts (land that is now Easton and Bethlehem) bordered land owned by William Allen, Pennsylvania chief justice, and Jeremiah Langhorne, Bucks County justice of the peace. The rest was, for the Penns' practical purposes, beginning to be conceived of as "Vacant Land."[47] The lottery was "frequently and Publickly declaimed" and never gained the acceptance of the Quakers.[48] Though thousands of acres were sold in the Forks, the projected profits never materialized.[49] A new strategy was needed.

John Penn returned to England to seek a buyer for Pennsylvania. Thomas Penn and James Logan sent William Parsons into the Forks secretly to survey more tracts for James Steel, William Allen, and others. Penn began selling five-hundred-acre tracts in the Forks, keeping the most advantageously situated for himself.[50] Warranted, secretly surveyed, and paid for, still these acreages could not be patented, that is, become profitable to their purchasers, until the land became clear of Indian claims. This policy guided the Land Office from the colony's beginning. Its practicality was sound, since settlers generally refused to pay for land cumbered by indigenous claims. So James Logan drafted a treaty between Pennsylvania and the Iroquois Confederacy, which included these words:

> We desire further of our Brethren Onas and James Logan never to buy any land of our cousins the Delawares and others who we treat as cousins. They are people of no virtue and have nowhere a fire burning and deal very often unjust with our friends and brethren the English. Let it be manifest to all people that if it so be the Delawares our cousins offering to sell any lands to the Europeans that no Body may buy it of them, for they have no Land remaining to them; and if they offer to sell they have no good design.[51]

In October 1736, Logan entrusted Conrad Weiser, the province's most experienced Indian diplomat, to take this and another document to the Iroquois and persuade them to sign and simultaneously release all claims to land lying along the Delaware and its tributaries. "These nations," Logan wrote of the Iroquois, "have in reality no manner of Pretence to any Land on ye waters of Delaware." "It was understood that they laid no manner of Claim to the Lands on Delaware River or on the Waters running into" it.[52] But James Logan wanted legal documents by which the Iroquois released all claims to Delaware Valley land, together with their promise "that they must not Assign transfer release or in any way Set or let or make over their Right or Claim to any of the Lands within ye bounds of the Govern [en]t of the Province of Pennsylvania to any Persons whatsoever whether white people or Indians other than to the Proprietors of the Said Province the Children of Wm Penn or those who act under them in their behalf."[53] Knowing that the Iroquois made no claims to the Forks or Minisink, Logan, with Weiser's expert help, was carefully laying a legal framework for dispossessing the Delaware and paving the way for regulated settlement and proprietorial profits. He was simultaneously enlisting the support of the powerful Iroquois against the likelihood of conflict with the Delaware. Logan instructed Weiser to induce the Iroquois to honor the Pennsylvania "Law that no person shall purchase Lease or rent Land or its Timber or Grass of any Indian but the Proprietors alone and those whom they appoint," and thereby minimize any chance the Delawares might have to "procure from" the Iroquois "some Colour of a Grant by which they may Still Claim" Lehigh Valley land.[54] By getting the Iroquois to quitclaim the Forks, Logan could technically maintain William Penn's policy of negotiating with the Indians and simultaneously avoid the Delawares, who had thus far spurned his efforts to obtain clear title to the Lehigh Valley. Logan's directions to Weiser clarify this motive.

> The reason to be given for . . . their not making any Grants to the Indians further than to allow them to live on the Land is this: that the five nations are our Brethren honest wise discreet and understanding men and we can treat with them with pleasure but the others are weak and too often knavish . . . Pesquiootomen Nootamis and the like to whom we are always very kind & take great care of them as of ourselves that they may in no point be abused yet we are not willing to enter upon Treaties with them as with our Brethren of the five nations for whom we keep our fire and therefore would treat with them only in behalf of all or any of the others. And all this should be said on presenting the Belt. If more will

sign the Deed they may and witness it thy self with some others one or two white men.[55]

Knowing it would be hard to persuade the Iroquois to quitclaim land to which the Delaware, not they, had rightful claim, Logan wanted Weiser to emphasize that "they do not grant us any Land on Delaware therefore observe to them that this is not at all intended by it but they only release and quit all their Claim there and as they make none it is in reality nothing & yet may prevent disputes hereafter." If this line of reasoning was not persuasive, Logan included "ten pounds more wrapt within the Belt to be aplied or not as there shall be occasion." Weiser was instructed to "be very kind to them and let them go to Shamokin perfectly well Satisfied," though "guarded against the Impressions the Indians from Delaware will endeavour to make on them there."[56]

On October 27, 1736, Weiser sent word to Logan that after "consideration from morning till night," and evidently aided in their deliberations by rum courtesy of the proprietors, "15 of the chiefs have syned and four of their younger people have syned for Witness and two of my neighbours besides me." Weiser added that "it went very hard about syning over their right upon delaware because they sayd they had nothing to doe there about the land, they were afraid they should doe any thing a mis to their gosens [cousins] the delawars."[57] Cunningly, secretly James Logan and Conrad Weiser had obtained crucial Iroquois cooperation in pressuring Delawares in the Forks finally to relinquish their claims. Those who admire James Logan's diplomacy in this affair are Iroquois-centric. His brilliant but duplicitous actions proved devastating to the Delawares.[58]

A strange series of events occurred in Philadelphia on May 29, 1737, a few months before the Walking Purchase was executed in September. Two upper Forks traders, Huguenot Nicholas Dupui and Daniel Broadhead, battled for exclusive rights to the upper Delaware Indian trade. Both tried to ally themselves with the Delaware sachem Lapowinzo, destined to join three other Delawares in marking the August 25, 1737, quitclaim used to authorize the walk. In a meeting with Thomas Penn, Dupui showed the proprietor a petition signed by Lapowinzo and forged marks of other Delawares, asserting that Broadhead's April 5, 1737, land warrant for six hundred acres "beyond the Blue Mountains" in the Minisink should be recalled since he had "done them much wrong and cheated them very grossly." Dupui, meanwhile, "had been their trusty and loving

Lapowisna, by Hesselius. Courtesy of The Historical Society of Pennsylvania Collection, Atwater Kent Museum of Philadelphia.

friend and had often redressed and relieved them from the wrongs
done to them by the said Broadhead and therefore they had given
him the same tract of land that they might have the liberty to give
away what was their own without molestation and that they were resolved that neither Daniel Broadhead nor any others should settle
the said land in peace except Nicholas Depue," who was obviously
the author of the petition. The proprietor summoned Broadhead,
who happened also to be in Philadelphia. With Dupui, Broadhead,
and Lapowinzo present, Thomas Penn had the petition "read by
paragraphs and rendered into the Indian language." Lapowinzo
said that Dupui had "told him he must sign it, which he did, but the
other Indians whose names are also to the petition were not there,
except one. . . . That he knew nothing of the contents of the petition, nor had anything to say against Daniel Broadhead, only that
some matchcoats which he had from him were not so good as he
expected."[59]

Knowing what occurred next, one can almost sense the machina-
tions of Thomas Penn's mind as he listened to this testimony in the
context of wondering how to induce the Delawares to relinquish the
Forks. The dispute existed between Broadhead (whose warrant,
though cumbered by Delaware claims, was legal) and Dupui, who
was blatantly using Delawares in his scheme to usurp Broadhead's
market position. Both Broadhead and Dupui drop out of the minutes, however, as Penn seizes the opportunity to cajole Lapowinzo
into the Walking Purchase. According to minutes of the meeting,
after Lapowinzo finished his report, Penn told him by interpreter
that William Penn

> had always been kind to the Indians and purchased and paid them for
> their lands, he did not take it well that they should sell any to other peo-
> ple because it was unjust to do so. A law of the Province was provided to
> prevent the same and render such purchases void and therefore to con-
> tinue the friendship that has always subsisted between the Proprietor
> and the Indians, it would be necessary to fix the bounds of the former
> purchase by walking out the distances according to the deeds passed by
> the Indians to the late Proprietor.

Persuaded in part by lavish gifts, Lapowinzo agreed but predicted a
protest from Delawares led by Nutimus.[60]

During the summer of 1737, then, a Pennsylvania settler forged
marks and convinced Delawares to sign a document, though they

"knew nothing of the contents." Dupui's petition failed to get Broadhead evicted, but it may have inspired Thomas Penn, whose agent, James Logan, invited Nutimus, Manawkyhickon, Lapowinzo, and Tishecunk to Stenton, his estate north of Philadelphia, for an August 25–26, 1737, meeting to discuss the purchase one more time.

The Delaware sachems arrived with information from their elders that a 1686 agreement had been reached, "but without making the Indians any Pay for the Lands."[61] Thomas Penn again began his entreaty with conciliating remarks and reminders of the Delawares' goodwill toward his father for his kindness to them. Again the proprietor presented the August 1686 document as evidence that land north of the 1682 purchase had been not only negotiated but paid for by Penn, and all that remained was for the sachems to agree to release their claims. Depositions from Joseph Wood and William Biles were presented as proof that the 1686 document was a true copy of an actual 1686 deed that had been signed and paid for.

The Delaware speaker Manawkyhickon acknowledged the mutually satisfying negotiations Delawares enjoyed with William Penn. He guardedly said "he should be sorry if after this mutual love and friendship anything should arise that might create the least misunderstanding." He offered a belt of wampum and an explanation. The Delawares were hesitant to agree to terms because they did not understand "how the lines mentioned in the deeds from Sayhoppy and his Brother Chiefs are to run."[62] Andrew Hamilton then drafted an inaccurate map intended to create misunderstanding, "to shew and explain to the Indians the Boundaries of the said Land and the Course of the one and Half Day's Walk, which was to determine and fix the Extent or Head Line of that Purchase to the Northward."[63]

Neither Penn nor Allen nor any interested Pennsylvanians wanted the Delawares to comprehend the vastness of the land they sought. So the map depicted the Delaware River from its west-east bend east of Philadelphia to its turn northward. It represented the Spruce Tree on the Delaware bank, and Neshaminy Creek, between which the northern boundary of the 1682 purchase extended east to west. Farther north, though greatly compressed in scale, the map showed the "West Branch Delaware River," or the Lehigh, flowing into the Delaware. Between these two lines it purposely did not represent Tohickon Creek. A dotted line was added to give an impression of the direction the walk would take, jutting east from Neshaminy and

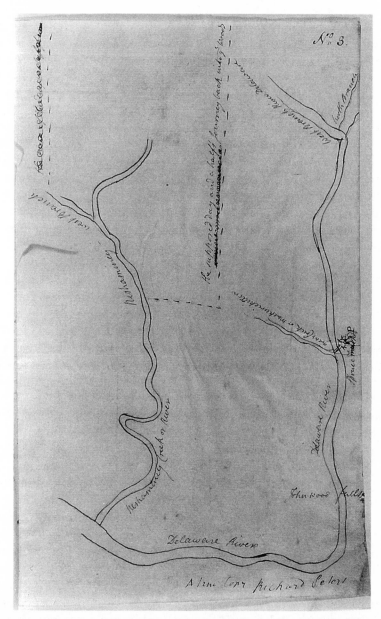

Distorted map by Andrew Hamilton, 1736, Historical Society of Pennsylvania. Notice that Tohickon Creek, the boundary in question, is missing. It should be depicted between the spruce tree and the Lehigh River. Moreover, the direction of the walk on the map is more northerly than the actual northwesterly walk, which tended away from the Delaware River. Courtesy Historical Society of Pennsylvania.

then abruptly north toward the Lehigh, disguised as Tohickon Creek.[64]

As William Allen remembered the events of August 25, 1737, after the four sachems had the map explained to them and "fully considered what had been then shewn and said to them, they declared themselves fully satisfied and convinced of the Truth thereof and that the lands mentioned in the said Deeds had been fairly sold by their Ancestors to the said William Penn; and that they were willing to join in a full Confirmation thereof to the said Proprietors."[65] The minutes of the meeting agree but reveal how the deceptive image disguised the duplicitous proprietorial intentions. After conferring, Manawkyhickon "said that all that they had heard touching the said Deed and now seeing the lines in it laid down they are sufficiently convinced of the truth thereof, and that the lands therein mentioned were sold by their ancestors to William Penn, and that they have no objection, but are willing to join in a full and absolute confirmation of the said sale." The sachems marked a document that confirmed the 1686 deed draft and called for the walk to be made "forthwith."

Hamilton's map holds the key. It seems to have been carefully prepared to convey the impression to the sachems that all they were relinquishing was land below Tohickon Creek, as the Delawares had been willing to do since 1686. The misleading scale, the conspicuous absence of Tohickon Creek, and the dotted line of the projected walk, which was much closer and more nearly parallel to the general course of the Delaware River than the 1735 trial walk—these features almost certainly caused the sachems to think that what the map showed as the Lehigh River was actually Tohickon Creek. And since the Lehigh (disguised as Tohickon) and the dotted line showing the course of "the approved day and a half's journey back into ye woods" both ended near the top of the map, it appeared that the proprietors were finally asking for the land north of the 1682 survey and south of Tohickon.

Thus what might appear to be waffling by the Delawares was actually informed negotiation, which they thought would ensure that their terms would be met to the very letter. These were the same terms to which their ancestors persuaded William Markham to commit in 1682. The August 1737 meeting ended with Delawares' obtaining a promise from Thomas Penn. "As the Indians and white people have ever lived together in a good understanding, they the Indians would request that they may be permitted to remain on their present settlements and plantations tho within that purchase, without being molested." Penn repeated his earlier assurances on this point "and confirmed them."[66]

As long as Delawares maintained rights to the Forks landscape, the Penns could not profit from their premature sales to Allen and others who were anxious to benefit from the rapid expansion of settlement into the Forks and Minisink. So the proprietors made promises they did not intend to keep. Their agents crafted documents, visual aids, and offered verbal explanations that, when presented to the sachems in veiled terms, persuaded Delawares to relinquish title to Bucks County land, well south of the Forks. Once marked by the sachems, the 1737 quitclaim proved to be perfectly ambiguous to suit proprietorial aims. It enabled the Penns to capitalize on the land speculation so far advanced in the Forks and the Minisink. Best of all, the proprietors and their agents now had legal title, official papers with ancient precedents that gave them unquestioned authority with everyone from the influential English itinerant George Whitefield to German Moravians to the privy councilors of King George II of England and his Deputy for Indian Affairs in North America, Sir William Johnson.

All pieces of the proprietorial conspiracy came together at Stenton—the land already surveyed and sold, the preliminary walk with its reconnaissance that the Forks could be encompassed in a day and a half, depositions that transformed a preliminary deed for an aborted 1686 deal for land below Tohickon into an already purchased tract that extended far north of that creek. Finally an illusory map caused the sachems to think they were releasing claim to land below Tohickon but not Forks or Minisink land. Cartographer Mark Monmonier explained, "Land ownership in the profane European sense of buying, selling, inheriting, recording, and taxing was an alien concept. American Indians, who considered the land sacred and not 'ownable,' never developed a formal cartography focused on boundaries and surveys. This lack of maps—really a lack of what the European invaders recognized as maps—was one of the many technological disadvantages that made the conquest of the New World not only quick and easy but also morally right in the minds of the colonists."[67]

Satisfied that their interests were protected and pleased to facilitate good relations with their "Honourable Brethren John and Thomas Penn" because they were sons of the sachems' "good Friend and Brother William Penn," Manawkyhickon, Lappawinzo,

Tishecunk, and Nutimus added their marks to a document they did not write and could not read. It confirmed the 1686 document, even to preserving the blank spaces, the eventual contents of which would determine the direction of the walk and the bearing of the survey line to be drawn from its end to the Delaware River. This confirmation deed of 1737 had another feature that set it apart from the 1682 deed, which stipulated that both settlers and Delawares "may freely pass Throug[h]" the lands held by the other "with out molestio[n]."[68] It betrayed Thomas Penn's verbal, recorded promise that Delawares could remain on the landscape "tho within that purchase, without being molested."[69] The 1737 document was distinctly different in tone, comprehensive and final:

> The Delaware Indians fully clearly and absolutely remove, release, and forever quit claim unto the said John Penn, Thomas Penn and Richard Penn all our Right, Title, Interest, and Pretensions whatsoever of in or to the said Tract or Tracts of Land and every Part and Parcell thereof so that neither we nor any of us or our children shall or may at any Time hereafter have challenge, claim or demand any Right Title Interest or Pretensions whatsoever of in or to the said Tract or Tracts of Land or any part thereof, but of and from the same shall be excluded and forever debarred.[70]

The Penns and James Logan had worked hard and waited impatiently for the sachems to mark that paper. They needed it to legitimize their activities in the Forks and Minisink, but perhaps even more to provide insurance against the outrage their actions would generate once the sachems understood the duplicity. For now, though, all that remained was to prosecute the prearranged walk. Thomas Penn sent instructions to Bucks County sheriff Timothy Smith to see the job through expeditiously.

On September 19, 1737, two of the three walkers of 1735—James Yeates and Edward Marshall—accompanied by Solomon Jennings, one of hundreds of settlers now living in the Forks, and supply horses, Indian companions, Sheriff Smith, and Surveyor General Benjamin Eastburn, among others, set off behind Joseph Knowles's advance party (sent ahead to ensure efficient passage) on the trail blazed two years earlier. Inspired by the proprietors' promise of five hundred acres in the Forks for the walker who covered the most terrain, they walked fast, by all accounts, and surprised the Indians by going northwestward away from the Delaware River rather than parallel to it. They were well beyond Tohickon Creek when they stopped for lunch just south of the Blue Mountains and the Lehigh River. Jennings had quit, but Marshall and Yeates were forty-five miles from Wrightstown before they camped north of the Lehigh River. Thomas Furniss, who was riding alongside, noted that the party "lodged in the woods that night, and heard the shouting of the Indians," gathered at nearby Hockendocqua for a cantico.[71] On the second day Yeates became a casualty of the strenuous pace and difficult terrain, and he died a few weeks later, but by midafternoon on September 20, Edward Marshall had earned himself an English half crown by covering more than sixty miles, far more than the Delawares anticipated.[72] He and Sheriff Smith started for home at a much more leisurely pace. Surveyor General Benjamin Eastburn and his Bucks County deputies, Nicholas Skull and John Chapman, spent a week more taking advantage of the perfectly placed blanks in the 1686 draft and 1737 confirmation. They turned a survey line nearly perpendicular to the course of the walk rather than to the general course of the river. Thus the new bound intersected the river far to the northeast near the confluence of the Delaware and Lackawaxen rivers on the Pennsylvania–New York border.[73]

Very few unofficial documents of the Walking Purchase remain. Most of Thomas Penn's papers between July 1736 and November 1738 are conspicuously missing, and his agents were circumspect with their words. Receiver General James Steel penned one of few surviving letters material to the Walking Purchase survey. He wrote to Letitia Aubrey Penn, the proprietors' sister, in September 1737:

> The old Indian purchase was circumscribed according to the Deed produced and proved at Pennsbury when a treaty was held there in thy presence [in] 1682[6] & the surveyor general and thy nephew who attended the people that walked over the land—and afterwards continued their Journey from the upper point of the one & one half days walk to the River Delaware, which employed them about four days—informed us on their return home, that after they crossed the great Ridge of Mountains, they saw very little good, or even tolerable land fit for cultivation or Settlement. The course of their line not being prescribed in the deed of the purchase, the agent of the proprietaries instead of running by the nearest course to the river ran northeastward across the country, so as to strike the Delaware near the mouth of Lackawaxin Creek, thus extending far up the River, taking in all the Minisink Country and many thousand acres more, than if they had run by the nearest acres to the Delaware.[74]

The Historical Society of Pennsylvania (HSP), William Parsons Papers, field book of surveys, 1734–1736, pages 79–80. Though the October 25, 1736 survey documented on page 80 predated the September 1737 Walking Purchase, the northeastern bearing line of the Walking Purchase was entered earlier in the field book, but after the Walking Purchase survey was completed. Presumably the Walking Purchase survey was entered on page 79 in the field book, which had been left blank, to legitimize the surveys (like the one on page 80) conducted earlier.

One of few relevant Thomas Penn letters to escape censorship informed his brothers that the Walking Purchase "takes in as much ground as any person here ever expected." Even better, it did so "at no very great Expence." He added that "the Minutes of the Treaty are not settled in so exact a Manner as I shal[l] have them reduced to."[75]

The 1737 Walking Purchase circumscribed an area slightly smaller than Rhode Island[76]—1,110 square miles, 710,000 acres, including the land Thomas Penn had been selling since 1728, that William Allen and others had purchased and would now sell at extraordinary profits. Penn had not forgotten to reserve some for himself, his brothers, and his kin, nor to set aside a reservation called Indian

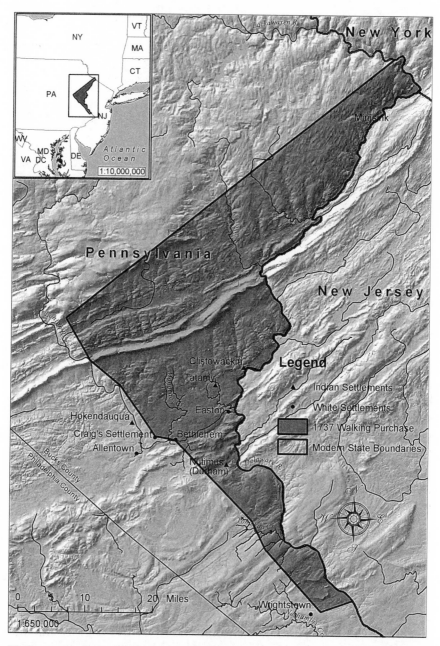

Modern map of the Walking Purchase by Brent Roper. Based on Benjamin Eastburn's 1737 map of the Walking Purchase (pix 2), the data in the field book of
William Parsons (pix 6) adjusted for magnetic declination, and a modern survey by
the author and John J. Harper, this is the most accurate map of the Walking Purchase to date.

Manor. The Penn heirs might have thought their fiscal troubles were behind them. But the Walking Purchase proved to be a new beginning of proprietary problems. Delaware interpreter Tunda Tatamy summarized:

> Manawkeyhicon who then resided at Wyoming went down to Philadelphia attended by Nutimus & sevl. Of the Fork Indians, at wch: time [1737] Manawkeyicon tho he had no Right to the Land was persuaded to sign a Writing whereby he conveyed over to ye Proprietaries as much Land as a man could walk over in a Day & half; Nutimus it is said was drawn in to Sign it tho' it does not appear that he ever recd any Consideration for it. They accordingly had the Land walked over by what ye Indians call ye hurry walk & instead of following the Course of the River as they ought, they had a Line laid out by the Compass by wch: they were enabled to travel over a Vast Extent of Country, & by this time People came fast to settle the Land in the Forks, so that in a short time it was full of Settlement & the Indians were oblig'd to remove farther back.[77]

As settlers arrived fast and thick to fill the Forks, they left little room, spatially or culturally, for Delawares, who were, politely put, obliged to remove.

The weapons of dispossession left strange wounds. No Delawares died as an immediate result of the Walking Purchase. There is no Wounded Knee in eastern Pennsylvania or a single Trail of Tears leading from there. Because the Delawares were dispossessed diplomatically, their protests politely ignored, the methods of nonviolent removal were memorialized as innocuous and civilized. Deeds, maps, negotiation paved the way for Pennsylvania's peaceable possession of Delaware lands. With these documents Pennsylvania officials created an undying legend of their innocence, founded on the overstated benevolence of William Penn. Beneath this idealized image, however, an insatiable demand for possession of the landscape portended the end of negotiated coexistence of Delawares and colonists.

6

No More Brothers and Friends

If this practice must hold why then we are No more Brothers and
Friends but much more like Open Enemies.
          —Delawares to Jeremiah Langhorne, January 3, 1741

DELAWARES CONSIDERED THE WALKING PURCHASE WILDLY UNJUST AND
complained of it from its execution. Their pleas were dismissed,
however, as alliance between Pennsylvania and the Iroquois Confederacy served as the mechanism for Delaware dispossession in the
wake of the 1737 walk. The Iroquois assertion of Delawares' inferior
status, a feminine status, served as the rationale for removal of Delawares. The significance of this gendered identity has been under-
stated, both in its potency as a weapon and in its power to elicit
resentment. Delawares responded to these aftereffects in varied
ways, often forging individual identities in place of more communal
consciousness. Just as often, Delawares rejected or modified identities prescribed by European colonists.

Past efforts to understand Delaware responses to the Walking Purchase grossly underestimated their resentment. One must rely on
proprietary reports of the Walking Purchase, whose authors alche-
mized unheeded Delaware complaints into unmade ones. Delawares
complained about the Walking Purchase and all the settlement that
preceded and followed it but were ignored, then silenced. For more
than a decade their frustrations were unheard. One Delaware account tells us that Braddock's 1755 defeat gave them a "favourable
Opportunity of taking Revenge" for the injustices of the Walking
Purchase.[1] As Delawares capitalized violently on that long-awaited
chance, surprised settlers and disingenuous Pennsylvania officials
wondered why the unreasonable and "savage" complainers had
failed to speak up sooner. The idea that Delawares were content with
the Walking Purchase until officious Quakers coaxed them to com-

plain originated in the official Pennsylvania reports designed to cover the impropriety. Informed but less invested eighteenth-century authorities locate blame with the Pennsylvania proprietors and their agents.[2] Official reports paint a pervasive image of gullible, childish Delawares easily duped and easily pacified, who inexplicably unleashed a torrent of death and destruction with some encouragement from the French.

Delawares "made no complaint about the method of the walk for twenty years, and then only when they were seeking a *casus belli* after the fact," wrote Julian Boyd.[3] But Delawares began complaining as soon as the walkers crossed Tohickon Creek and had not stopped when the Moravian missionary John Heckewelder heard them late in the eighteenth century.[4] Sassoonan complained to James Logan in 1728 that "Christians settle on lands that the Indians have never been paid for."[5] Before the Walking Purchase became an issue at negotiations in which Quakers assisted Delawares, two Moravians heard Delawares complain that since "ye walk was made . . . ye Indians were then & ever since dissatisfied with ye manner in wch it was done."[6] Teedyuscung, a nephew of Nutimus's and his successor as sachem, continued to complain eloquently in the generation after the Walking Purchase. A source partisan to the proprietors noted that "about the year 1756, or rather long before, the Indians under Tediuscung made loud complaints against the proprietaries of Pennsylvania for defrauding them of their lands."[7] In 1757 William Parsons informed Provincial Secretary Richard Peters that "Teedyuscung himself as well as the other Indians has been frequently heard to say that the land whereon Easton stands is his land."[8] The most informed local historian, A. D. Chidsey, wrote accurately, "These Indians continually complained to the authorities that not only were settlers moving into their land at the Forks of the Delaware, but that the Proprietaries were selling land in this territory."[9]

Francis Jennings exposed the facile logic—that nonviolent responses to the Walking Purchase meant Delawares must have been satisfied.[10] Rather, the Penns and their agents worked to quell the complaints and employed Iroquois cooperation to humiliate and silence Delawares. When Sassoonan complained in 1728, James Logan assured the Delaware sachem that William Penn made it a rule "never to suffer any lands to be settled by his people, till they were first purchased of the Indians; that his commissioners had followed the same rule."[11] Logan betrayed the falsehood of this and similar statements in his correspondence with the Penn heirs. Reporting a surveying foray into the Forks, Logan wrote in December 1727 that "the Indians would suffer no manner of survey to be made there on any account whatsoever. There never was any pretense of a purchase made on thy Father's account within thirty miles of the nearest of these Indian settlements."[12]

In 1702 Logan himself bought five hundred acres of land in the present Solebury Township. Meanwhile he and the other commissioners sold 5,000 acres above Tohickon Creek to John Streiper in 1701, 580 acres to William Beeks in 1702, and 2,500 to John White a year later.[13] These men were patient and there was no great pressure to clear their tracts of Delaware cumbrance while William Penn remained alive. That changed after his death in 1718, dramatically so in 1730 when Penn's sons gained control of Pennsylvania. Traders and settlers made significant inroads into the Upper Delaware Valley in the 1720s and 1730s. Nicholas Dupui, a French Huguenot, bought part of William Allen's ten thousand Upper Delaware Valley acres on September 10, 1733.[14] Daniel Broadhead received a warrant for six hundred acres from Thomas Penn as the Walking Purchase was in the offing. At least one trader, John Mathers, preceded Dupui and Broadhead.[15] Land warrants were issued to Edward Marshall (destined to be the sole finisher of the brisk walk of 1737) and his brothers in 1733 north of Tohickon Creek. The warrants were patented in 1738 after Marshall's service to the proprietors gave them confidence enough to issue patents on Delaware lands.[16] Scots-Irish settlers encroached on lands at the Forks of the Delaware and Lehigh rivers in 1728. Their first substantial settlement, Craig's Settlement, grew in what is presently Allentown. By 1731 it included a Presbyterian church. Other Scots-Irish settlers took up land northeast of Craig's, establishing the Martin's Creek settlement beginning in 1728. These settlers infiltrated the Forks before the Walking Purchase and began the telling process of putting their possessive names on the landscape.[17] After the Walking Purchase proprietary agents granted patents and investors traded acreages in a flurry of transactions that included Marshall's patents. Land long held by William Allen, the Penn heirs, or Penn agents like James Steel, who were in the know regarding the Walking Purchase and positioned to take advantage of rising land prices, yielded enormous returns.

Increasingly intrusive colonization followed these early investments. In 1735, Allen paid Letitia Penn Aubrey, William Penn's daughter, five hundred pounds for five thousand acres in the Forks gifted her by her brothers. Anticipating the settlement of this land,

Nathaniel Irish built a mill and cleared farmland at the confluence of Saucon Creek and the Lehigh River, where he managed Allen's local real estate transactions. The most notable sale involved the English itinerant George Whitefield. "Mr. Seward, Mr. Whitefield's traveling companion, had bought a piece of land of about 5000 acres in the forks of the Delaware, which was named Nazareth." Between April 30 and May 4, 1740, Whitefield paid Allen £2,200 for the land. Allen realized a 440 percent profit on his five-year investment. Whitefield's contacts with the Moravian bishop Peter Boehler in Savannah, Georgia, led to an agreement for the Moravians to build a school for free blacks on Whitefield's land. They "moved on the land to the forks of the Delaware" beginning in May 1740, "just about in the place where the Nazareth Plantation is now located. At that time a fairly large Indian town [Meniolagomekah] stood there."[18]

Doctrinal differences, exacerbated by Scots-Irish settlers in the Forks opposed to Moravian immigration, brought the cooperative venture to an abrupt end, but the Moravians determined to stay in the area and establish settlements from which to operate their ambitious educational, industrial, and proselytizing ventures. Nathaniel Irish interested Boehler and then his replacement, Bishop David Nitschman, in a five-hundred-acre Allen tract situated beautifully astride Monocacy Creek and bordered on the south by the Lehigh River in the heart of present Bethlehem. When Whitefield's benefactor died, "he could no longer retain the land" at Nazareth, and the Moravians were positioned to negotiate for the whole five thousand acres on good terms, "and so," Bishop Boehler said, "Nazareth came into the hands of the congregation, and the Brethren who formerly were day laborers there and exiles, afterwards became the owners and inhabitants of the place." They were sure "Der Heiland, or the Savior, was behind it all."[19]

From a stock of nearly a dozen pioneers, supplemented by successive waves of immigrants, the Moravian settlements grew and thrived. They built mills and cultivated farms under the direction of the farsighted Bishop Augustus Gotlieb Spangenburg. When Count Zinzendorf was in Pennsylvania from 1741 to 1743 he oversaw Moravian settlement and proselytizing. Moravian tradition recalls the 1740s as a time of love feasts, abundant harvests, and "Indians who were friendly, and came to the farms on brief visits. They even helped in the harvesting and gave good service." But sometimes "lurking in the vicinity" were "wild Indians."[20] The Moravians and other Europeans had referred to these as "savages" and "heathen" all along, but Delawares became increasingly categorized by Europeans newly in possession of the landscape, leaving fewer possibilities.[21]

The late eighteenth-century Moravian cooper and sometimes missionary John Heckewelder thought that while Europeans were settling Forks lands, Delawares were protesting the encroachment. "They loudly exclaimed against the white people for settling in this part of the country, which had not yet been legally purchased of them, but, as they said, had been obtained by fraud." Pennsylvania officials gave no heed and urged the Moravians to do likewise.[22] But an impulse to evangelize Native Americans drove Moravian settlement. They desired to convert Delawares, not overtly displace them. This had mixed consequences for Delawares. On one hand it increased the potency of some Delawares in negotiations, since Moravians determined, in William Penn fashion, to coexist and to pay the Delawares for lands already purchased legally from William Allen. Heckewelder noted that Zinzendorf "paid them out of his private purse the whole of the demand which they made in the height of their ill temper, and moreover gave them permission to abide on the land, at their village, where they had a fine large peach orchard, as long as they should think proper."[23] Heckewelder's description bears some resemblance to the 1682 deed, drafted in part to codify peaceful coexistence of Quakers and Delawares by assuring that "we may freely pass through any of their lands, as well that which is not purchased as that which is, without molestation as they do quietly amongst us."[24] Tishcohan (or Captain John) negotiated for and received compensation from the Moravians for his huts, orchard, and grains and retained the power to enjoy the fruit of his labors.[25] But the primary documentation of this negotiation sounds more like the 1737 confirmation of the Walking Purchase. Moravians collaborated with the Pennsylvania government to increase settlement in the Walking Purchase, believing that if Delawares could be "Cooped up into a narrow Compass and Subdued," conversions would follow. They joined purposes with the Pennsylvania government to "dispossess the Indians in Nazareth."[26] Just prior to the July 1742 meeting in Philadelphia at which the Iroquois demanded that Delawares vacate the Walking Purchase, Moravian agents agreed with the Pennsylvania government on terms that would allow Tishcohan to remain. "If the Government can convince the Indians at Nazareth," including Tishcohan, "that the land . . . has been purchased and warranted to us . . . we are willing that the said Captain continue his

Tishcohan, by Hesselius. Courtesy of The Historical Society of Pennsylvania Collection, Atwater Kent Museum of Philadelphia.

habitation on our land, and that he enjoy the use of all the land he has hitherto cleared. We will also consider him as our tenant."[27] That concession suggests how much power Delawares had lost as well as what they retained. On December 26, 1742, Tishcohan told the Moravians he intended to "withdraw and move away."[28]

While Moravians settled Bethlehem, down the Lehigh River John and Thomas Penn were planning their own town, Easton, and imposing manors and baronies on the Forks landscape, making it as much like the mother country as they could. Ever since their visit to the confluence of the Lehigh and Delaware rivers in late 1734 or early 1735, the Penns coveted the place and envisioned a commercial center there.[29] To surveyors anticipating the Walking Purchase, the Penns specified that the area immediately northwest of the confluence be reserved for them. Wanting this Delaware hunting territory for their own uses, the Penn heirs thought of accommodating

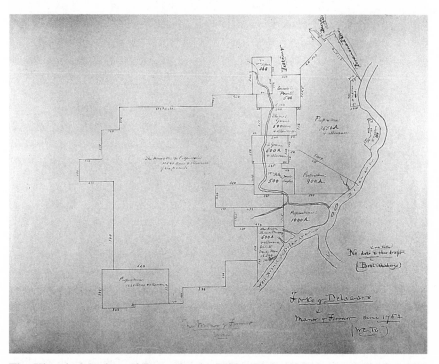

The Historical Society of Pennsylvania (HSP), Forks of Delaware and Manor of Fermor, circa 1752. This map of the present site of Easton, Pennsylvania shows land surveyed for the proprietors beginning in 1734. Tattemy's land is designated near the top.

the Delawares in terms of fitting them into English property ways by designating an Indian Manor, located up the Lehigh beyond lands already surveyed for paying customers. If Delawares took advantage of this largesse, they left by the 1750s, perhaps when hostilities rose in the summer of 1755. With an eye for revenue generation, Thomas Penn directed Richard Peters in 1759, "as there is no probability of the Indians coming back to the Indian Manor. I think if tenants offer it should be let."[30]

The coincidence of Moravian settlement and even less Delaware-friendly developments demonstrates that when the Penns and their agents acted as if Delawares were a nuisance, they became so. Even then Delawares sought redress of grievances through colonial channels. Surely litigious colonists could not object to nonviolent Delaware complaints. Or perhaps that was precisely the problem. That supposed savages did not react savagely until no alternatives remained gained them a reputation for impetuosity rather than patience, gullibility rather than civility. It took a conspiratorial and offensive disregard for Delaware territoriality, exacerbated by condescending refusals to redress the situation, or even to hear the case, to evoke Delaware violence.

When initial complaints about the Walking Purchase went unheard, Delawares gave no legitimacy to the walk. So well situated to speculate in Forks lands, William Allen became giddy at the profits to be made.[31] When the Land Office began issuing patents to justify Allen's optimism, Delawares were no longer able simply to ignore the Walking Purchase. So in January 1740 Delawares filed a formal complaint with the Pennsylvania chief justice and upper Bucks County resident Jeremiah Langhorne, citing abuses by encroaching settlers. "If this practice must hold why then we are No more Brothers and Friends but much more like Open Enemies," the Delawares said.[32]

Harking back to Tammany's successful aggression in response to unrestrained Bucks County settlement in the 1680s, the angry appeal threatened violence if settlement was not arrested forthwith, implying Iroquois alliance and support. Governor George Thomas issued a condescending response. He feigned astonishment at Delaware demands to be paid for lands within the bounds of the Walking Purchase and urged Nutimus to "consider well what you do." Thomas assured the Delaware that in case of any conflict, the English enjoyed numerical superiority. Even better, Thomas intimated, the Penn government was allied with the Iroquois Confederacy.[33]

Unknown to Delaware sachems Sassoonan and Nutimus, Conrad Weiser's execution of James Logan's 1736 alliance treaties forged what Jennings aptly described as an Iroquois hammer and a Pennsylvania anvil.[34] Delawares were situated in the middle. Having been outwitted by Nutimus in 1736 negotiations for Delaware land, James Logan might have reveled in the knowledge that he could call Nutimus's bluff. Not quite a year earlier, Logan authored secretive diplomatic missives that Conrad Weiser persuaded Iroquois representatives to mark. Thus, even as Nutimus threatened, Logan confidently relied on a solidified alliance between the Iroquois Confederacy and the Pennsylvania government, not the Delawares.

In response to Delaware complaints about the Walking Purchase, members of Sassoonan's band, together with Nutimus and his cohorts, met representatives of the Iroquois Confederacy and the Pennsylvania government in Philadelphia during July 1742. Sassoonan sent word, explaining "that he lives in the middle between" the Iroquois and Pennsylvania and "desires to have the paths that lead to both places" open to him. Nutimus arrived complaining of "being cheated and abused" and hoped to have his grievances redressed.[35] Both were sorely disappointed and humiliated when the Pennsylvania-Iroquois alliance unexpectedly coerced Delaware removal from the Forks by a show of physical force and rhetoric that redefined the gendered relations between Iroquois and Delawares.

On July 12, 1742, Canassatego, the Onondaga orator, spoke to a gathering that included "sundry Chiefs of the six Nations," as well as "Sassoonan and Delawares" with "Nutimus and fork Indians" with the "Honble George Thomas," the Penns' lieutenant governor; James Logan; and others of the Provincial Council in attendance. Canassatego wasted no time before raising the issue of "the Misbehavior of our Cousins the Delawares with respect to their continuing to Claim and refusing to remove from some land on the River Delaware." The impressive Onondaga orator then rehearsed the by now familiar, though largely contrived history of the Walking Purchase, how Delawares had sold the land to Penn "upwards of fifty Years ago" and confirmed said sale in 1737. Canassatego's remarks were clearly motivated by Logan's diplomacy. The Onondaga spokesman's candor exposed some of the details expressed less baldly in Logan's letters. "You requested Us to remove them," Canassatego continued, speaking to Logan of the Delaware, "enforcing your Request with a String of Wampum." Citing the contrived map or "Draught of the Land in Dispute" and "several Writings to prove

the Charge" of illegitimate Delaware claims to the Forks, Canassatego informed all present that the Iroquois "have concluded to remove them, and Oblige them to go over the River Delaware, and to
quit all claim to any Lands on this side for the future."[36]

Canassatego then turned to the Delawares, held up a wampum
belt, and launched into a calculated speech recorded in the minutes
of the Provincial Council. Because of its influential and controver-
sial nature, it follows in full:

Cousins:
Let this Belt of Wampum serve to Chastize You; You ought to te taken by
the Hair of the Head and shak'd severely till you recover your Senses and
become Sober; you don't know what Ground you stand on, nor what you
are doing. Our Brother Onas' Case is very just and plain, and his Intentions to preserve friendship; on the other Hand your Cause is bad. Your
Heart far from being upright, and you are maliciously bent to break the
Chain of friendship with our Brother Onas. We have seen with our Eyes
a Deed signed by nine of your Ancestors above fifty Years ago for this
very Land, and a Release Sign'd not many Years since by some of your-
selves and Chiefs now living to the Number of 15 or Upwards. But how
came you to take upon you to Sell Land at all? We conquer'd You, we
made Women of you, you know you are Women, and can no more sell
Land than Women. Nor is it fit you should have the Power of Selling
Lands since you would abuse it. This Land that you Claim is gone
through Your Guts. You have been furnished with Cloaths and Meat and
Drink by the Goods paid you for it, and now You want it again like Children as you are. But what makes you sell Land in the Dark? Did you ever
tell Us that you had sold this Land? Did we ever receive any Part, even
the Value of a Pipe Shank, from you for it? You have told Us a Blind story
that you sent a Messenger to Us to inform Us of the Sale but he never
came amongst Us, nor we never heard any thing about it. This is acting
in the Dark, and very different from the Conduct of our six Nations observe in their Sales of Land. On such Occasions they give Publick Notice
and invite all the Indians of their united Nations, and give them a share
of the Present they receive for their Lands. This is the behaviour of the
wise United Nations, but we find you are none of our Blood. You Act a
dishonest part not only in this but in other Matters. Your Ears are ever
Open to slanderous Reports about our Brethren. You receive them with
as much greediness as Lewd Women receive the Embraces of Bad Men.
And for all these reasons we charge You to remove instantly. We don't
give you the liberty to think about it. You are Women; take the Advice of
a Wise Man and remove immediately. You may return to the other side
of Delaware where you came from, but we don't know whether, Consid-

ering how you have demean'd your selves, you will be permitted to live
there, or whether you have not swallowed that Land down your Throats
as well as the Land on this side. We, therefore, Assign you two Places to
go—either to Wyomin or Shamokin. You may go to either of these
Places, and then we shall have you more under our Eye, and shall see
how You behave. Don't deliberate, but remove away and take this Belt of
Wampum.[37]

Conrad Weiser interpreted this speech in English and Cornelius
Spring then retranslated it in Delaware. Canassatego then forbade
the Delawares or their descendants ever to deal in land transactions
again. Then in dramatization of his words, the Onondaga spokesman took Nutimus by the hair and forced him from the room as he
might a woman who had overstepped her prescribed bounds.

This crucial episode was key to the displacement of the Delawares.
Jane Merritt observed of the ordeal, the Iroquois "*created* a representation of women that, when wielded politically, disenfranchised and
dispossessed another of land."[38] The construction and manipulation
of this gendered identity have captured the attention of several
scholars, but no consensus obtains.[39] C. A. Weslager never satisfied
those who sought clear proof of the Iroquois *conquest* of the Delawares mentioned by Canassatego, but he cobbled together an impressive argument, showing that in "the relations between Delaware
and Five Nations, there constantly appear references to the 'man'
warrior versus the woman non-warrior and the superiority of the former." For example, a member of the Iroquois Confederacy thought,
"We the Mohawks are Men; we are made so from above, but the Delawares are Women, and under our Protection, and of too low a kind
to be Men."[40] Though they understandably tried to cast their subordination in the best possible terms, Delawares led by Sassoonan conceded as early as 1712 that the Iroquois "had subdued them" and
"had told them they were as Women only and desired them to plant
corn and mind their own private business" while the Iroquois
"would take care of what related to war and peace."[41]

A generation of Iroquois-friendly scholarship, sensitive to cultural
constructions and ethnographic data but too inclined to discover
empowered minorities, favors the view that the Delawares were not
bested by the Iroquois after any fashion, but rather negotiated a gendered relationship in which the Iroquois fought and defended while
Delawares pacified, or served, symbolically, as corporate women.
Delaware status is thus elevated by a supposed preference of the pre-

scribed feminine role of peacemaker over the masculine role of warrior. And the Iroquois do not seem as chauvinist as Europeans. This view accommodates the pervasive evidence of a gendered relationship between the Iroquois and Delawares without making the Iroquois seem unattractively condescending or casting Delawares as weak. Historiographically it gives eighteenth-century Delawares, as women, agency and remarkable autonomy that they did not have historically. Empirically this interpretation became privileged because of thin evidence for an Iroquois military conquest and because favored interpretations of gender roles within the Iroquois Confederacy do not support Canassatego's chauvinist claims.[42]

Jennings presented the most substantial argument against Iroquois conquest of the Delawares. He suspects censorship in recorded speeches of Delaware sachems Sassoonan and Scollitchy. If he is right, the two speeches support his argument that early eighteenth-century Delawares considered themselves peers of, not vassals to, the Iroquois. This unclear evidence does not prove that Delawares were not subordinate to Iroquois by 1700, but only suggests that Delawares refused to consider themselves subordinates. On this evidence, Jennings dismissed Canassatego's feminization of the Delaware as "oratorical fancy," suggesting that the Onondaga spokesman knowingly fabricated an Iroquois conquest of Delawares. To Jennings, Canassatego evoked the imagery of women as signifying conquered Delawares subservient to the Iroquois Confederacy simply as part of his obligation to the Pennsylvania Provincial Council, though the charges were without historical foundation. But Jennings made minimal use of evidence that supports Iroquois dominion if not violent conquest, which was the favored view of the Moravian missionary and ethnographer David Zeisberger and following him by John Heckewelder.[43]

Sassoonan's 1712 concession that the Iroquois "had subdued" the Delawares and "told them they were as Women only and desired them to plant corn and mind their own private business" is missing from Jennings's analysis.[44] Moreover, minutes of the 1718 transfer of Delaware Valley land to the proprietors has Sassoonan remembering "when he was but Small their nation was look'd on as dependent on the five nations."[45] Without fully disclosing the significance of Sassoonan's statements, Jennings dismissed the reminiscence as relating to a short interlude between 1677 and 1681 framed by Delaware autonomy. That is speculative, but both Jennings and Sassoonan agree that, coincident with the founding of Pennsylvania,

Delawares asserted independence from the Iroquois in proportion
to their alliance with the Pennsylvania government.[46] For Sassoonan
anyway, when the Delawares became the "children of William
Penn," they stopped being "dependent on the five nations."[47]

Jane Merritt subtly argued for an interpretive dimension to the
1742 speech. Canassatego, she suggests, knowingly employed "specific European concepts of female gender, in which women could
not own and sell land, to delineate Delawares' subordinate position
in terms the Euramericans would clearly understand."[48] But there is
no evidence that Canassatego thought in terms of European gender
prescriptions or that he had to. Matrilineage notwithstanding, the
social roles of Iroquois and Delaware women were similar in many
ways to those of European women. European observers thought the
purpose of Delaware matrilineage was to protect against perceived
impure bloodlines, not primarily to empower women.[49] So though
Delaware women controlled domestic space and kinships, considering their social position advantageous partakes of what Cynthia Eller
persuasively characterized as a myth of matriarchal sociology.[50]

In Iroquois, Delaware, and English society men mocked other
men by likening them to women.[51] When Delaware men laughed at
and taunted Englishmen, calling them "a parcel of old women for
that they could not travel without loaded Horses and Waggons full
of Provisions," the laughers and the laughed-at understood.[52] But
these exchanges did not need to involve the English. When Mohawk
messengers visited western Delawares in the 1750s, the Delawares responded in language that clarifies the significance of the gendered
identity Canassatego evoked. "They looked upon themselves as
men, and would acknowledge no Superiority that any other Nation
had over them. We are Men, and are determined not to be ruled any
longer by you as Women; and we are determined to cut off all the
English, except those that may make their Escape from us in Ships;
so say no more to us on that Head, lest we cut off your private Parts,
and make Women of you, as you have done of us."[53] Though recorded by English colonists, this exchange was not intended for English ears and therefore singularly reveals one meaning gendered
identities held for Iroquois and Delaware Indians. Men acknowledged no one as superior to them. Women were to "say no more"
in certain situations, and under threat of punishments if they did.
When Canassatego feminized Nutimus in part by assaulting him, he
was at home in this culture.

The most peculiar aspect of the 1742 episode, as Merritt noted, is that there is no previous record of using such gendering as rationale for dispossession. Canassatego apparently did not create but *adapted* "a representation of women that, when wielded politically, disenfranchised and dispossessed another of land."[54] It proved to be a devastatingly potent weapon for forcing Delaware removal and therefore fostering Delaware resentment. Moreover, as Kathleen Brown has written about Virginia colonists and Powhatans, "The very process of confrontation between two groups with male-dominated political and religious systems may initially have strengthened the value of patriarchy for both."[55] Delaware women lost most in the contested gendering and overtly masculine reactions against it.

Provincial Secretary Richard Peters revealed much when he reported the event to Thomas Penn: "The Six Nations, at the instance of our Governor, have ordered the Delaware Indians to remove immediately off the Land in the Forks on pain of their highest displeasure."[56] Teedyuscung never forgot seeing Canassatego feminize his uncle and sachem Nutimus, a gendering he would have found emasculating, not flattering. Beginning in 1755, he and his followers asserted their masculinity. Meanwhile "people came fast to settle the Land in the Forks, so that in a short time it was full of Settlement & the Indians were oblig'd to remove farther back."[57]

The 1740s saw the Forks of the Delaware and Lehigh rivers fill with European settlers as Delawares retreated or took up tenant farming. Depending on which narrow option they chose, Delawares were increasingly characterized as "civilized" or "savage." Whether in settlers' minds Delawares were the type to lend a hand at harvest-time or to steal or worse was a function of the ways European settlers wanted to possess and use the landscape and how well Delawares accommodated. Whether Delawares remained civil in their protests or became violent was a function of their sense of power to control their lives. By the 1740s, that power had been diminished considerably.

7

Border Men, Civilized Indians, and Savages: Cultural Identities in the Wake of the Walking Purchase

> Perhaps it is hardly proper to call the Indians of Penn's Colony "Savages," for they were not really such until after the noted Walk, by which means they were deceived and cheated. But after 1737 they looked upon most of the whites as enemies and intruders.
>
> —A. B. Burrell, *Reminiscences of George La Bar*

> In 1742, ten years before the founding of Easton, that territory which now comprises Northampton and Lehigh Counties, was cleared of Indians. Locally speaking, the first step in the inevitable advance of civilization had been taken. The local Indians had started their westward march, and as the frontier was slowly pushed toward the setting sun, these Indians were irresistibly carried before it, although their resistance at times was savage and bloodthirsty.[1]
>
> —A. D. Chidsey, *A Frontier Village*

In THE MIDDLE DECADES OF THE EIGHTEENTH CENTURY, THE LAND THAT became Northampton County, Pennsylvania, in 1752 hosted a steady influx of "border men," increasingly "civilized" Indians, and fewer supposed "savages."[2] As German and especially Scots-Irish settlers poured into the area and most Delawares migrated out, these neat categories circumscribed the possibilities that remained. As survey lines followed by fences imposed ever narrower options for the Delaware Valley landscape, Delawares could choose only to become "civilized Indians" or to remain "savages." Thus, rendering frontier Pennsylvania civilized required "savages" to civilize—by converting to Christianity, learning to read, adopting European agricultural techniques, "improving" private land. Strangely, the radical transformation of Penn's woods into a civilized society also required violent bursts of savagery—scalping, plundering, murdering. Because both white settlers and Delawares engaged in these behaviors in the 1750s, solidifying the cultural categories of "civilized" and "savage" required a subtle, complex, largely unconscious process of racialization that helped make the anxieties of frontier life bearable and Penn's woods habitable, though the cost included further geographical and cultural displacement of Delawares.[3]

A few Delawares, typified by Tunda Tatamy, chose to stay in the Forks. They underwent a process of acculturation, which, for Tatamy, began well before the Walking Purchase was executed. Tatamy and his family converted to Presbyterianism and became the first Indians to own land in Pennsylvania under English law. They represent one strategy Delawares used to accommodate European colonization. For other Delawares, like Teedyuscung, the Walking Purchase meant a physical move away from the Forks and a combination of violent attacks against and partial accommodation to a society and culture that took land and tradition but gave desirable goods. Similarly, the Walking Purchase led some Delawares to appropriate portions of Moravian Christianity, which were adapted to meet the needs of Delawares in a long period of cultural transformation.[4] The Walking Purchase also evoked Delaware responses ranging from seething resentment of anything European to an ascetic mysticism admired by the Quaker John Woolman.

After Canassatego's 1742 demand that Delawares leave the Forks, many relocated to the Susquehanna River valley, where the angst-ridden Presbyterian missionary David Brainerd tried to minister to them in 1744. They were anxious, he reported, because "the white people had abused them and taken their land from them."[5] When he attempted to convert the few remaining Forks Delawares he found them resentful as well and worried that they would reject his message because of the abuse they endured at the hands of Christian settlers. Brainerd recorded in his journal that "the number of Indians in this place is but small; most of those that formerly belonged here, are dispersed, and removed to places farther back in the country. There are not more than ten houses hereabouts, that continue to be inhabited; and some of these are several miles distant from others."[6]

One of the few who both remained and listened to Brainerd was Tunda Tatamy. In 1733, while Delawares generally were negotiating for goods and using land as capital or skins as a medium of exchange, Tatamy applied for "a piece of land of about 300 Acres on the forks of Delaware" on March 24, 1733. Receiver General James Steel sent word to Bucks County Deputy Surveyor John Chapman to make a formal survey "with caution and by Consent of the Indians."[7] Tatamy acquired this acreage in the Forks as "consideration of services he had rendered as interpreter and messenger to the Indians."[8] Undoubtedly the land-rich and cash-poor Penns appreciated this settlement. Tatamy received a patent for his farm on April 28, 1738. A 1742 patent finally granted him the land in fee simple.[9]

Tatamy was not complicit in the proprietors' plans to possess the Forks. He viewed the Walking Purchase as a corrupt bargain. But his service as the Penns' guide and interpreter probably gave him knowledge of their designs, and there are obvious chronological connections between his land grant and the Walking Purchase. Tatamy's 1733 application preceded the purchase but was among the first applications granted by the Penns before they gained Delaware quitclaim to the land in 1737. The patent Tatamy received on that land in 1738 followed shortly after the walk. The patent removing all restrictions on Tatamy's land followed the 1742 conference in which the Iroquois pressured Delawares to remove from the Forks. By issuing this patent the Penns upheld Canassatego's demand that Delawares vacate the Forks while rewarding Tatamy for his service.

The curious note from Steel to Chapman, that Tatamy's survey should be conducted with consent of the Indians, leads one to wonder how Tatamy's adoption of English property ways shaped his identity during this tumultuous period. Moreover, one wonders what connections beyond coincidence with his property acquisition may inform Tatamy's conversion to Christianity. During the extended process of acquiring his farm, which lies in the heart of the Forks land encompassed by the walk, Tatamy, his Delaware wife, and his daughter and two sons became Presbyterians. Were they, by virtue of their special investiture of land rights, or by religious affiliation, or some combination of the two, no longer considered "the Indians"?

Count Nikolaus Ludwig Zinzendorf, patron of the fledgling United Brethren (Moravians) in Saxony, who lived in Pennsylvania from 1741 to 1743, kept a travel account that reveals some of the sociocultural transformation of the Upper Delaware Valley in the wake of the Walking Purchase. On July 26, 1742, Zinzendorf visited "Tatamy's reserve" and found him "farming in a small way on a grant of 300 acres given him by the Proprietaries' agents." Tatamy welcomed Zinzendorf and his entourage and entertained them with "an account of the mode of sacrifice practiced by his heathen brethren." The missionaries capitalized on the chance to speak of "the great sacrifice of the Lamb of God, made for the remission of sins." How their teaching resonated with Tatamy cannot be known. Zinzendorf noted only vaguely that Tatamy "professed Christianity." But fallout from the Philadelphia meeting of July 12, 1742, two weeks before Zinzendorf's visit to Tatamy, in which Canassatego ordered Delawares to move from the Forks, forced Tatamy to clarify his cultural identity over the next few years.[10]

Iroquois orders for removal of Forks Delawares in July 1742 led Tatamy, Captain John, and other Delawares to petition the Pennsylvania governor for permission to remain at the Forks. The appeal argued that remaining Forks Delawares intended to live the settled life of other Christians, harmoniously with settlers and in "enjoyment of the same Religion & Laws with them." Provincial Secretary Richard Peters, an ordained Anglican minister, doubted the sincerity of such Christianity and had the petitioners catechized. They were found lacking in Christian knowledge.[11] Peters was sure that "those rascals, the Delaware Fork Indians," were best described by the label "savage," an increasingly used weapon for rationalizing dispossession. Peters reported to Thomas Penn that the remaining Delawares only "pretend to be converted to the Calvinistical scheme of religion." What was worse, thought Peters, on their petition they "had the impudence to subscribe themselves, 'Your Honour's brethren in the Lord Jesus.'"[12] His condescension sprang from his denominational differences with the Delaware converts but more from his Eurocentrism. Peters did not question the Scots-Irish Presbyterian nor the German Reformed nor the Moravian immigrants to the Forks, who were as doctrinally contemptible. They, in fact, served Peters as a convenient category against which he could fashion Delaware otherness. Then, having racialized otherness as rationale for dispossession, Peters could welcome the foreigners as countrymen and build a prosperous colony with them.

Tatamy and a few others adopted the strategy of staying put geographically but migrating culturally toward an identity acceptable to most Pennsylvanians, if not Richard Peters. When David Brainerd arrived in the Forks in 1744, Tatamy became his interpreter. Brainerd recorded,

When I first employ'd him in this Business in the Beginning of Summer 1744, he was well fitted for his Work in regard of his Acquaintance with

the Indian and English Language, as well as with the Manners of both
Nations. And in regard of his desire that the Indians should conform to
the Customs and Manners of the English, and especially their manner
of living; But he seem's to have little or no Impression of Religion upon
his Mind, and in that Respect was very unfit for his Work.[13]

Brainerd wanted it noted on earth and in heaven that he "labour'd
under great disadvantages in addressing the Indians, for want of his
[Tatamy's] having an experimental, as well as more doctrinal Acquaintance with divine Truths."[14]

For Brainerd, true conversion included adoption of English property ways as well as Calvinism. In 1744, Tatamy already "appeared
very desirous that the Indians should renounce their Heathenish
Notions and Practices, and conform to the Customs of the Christian
World." All he lacked was "concern about his own Soul."[15] Of Delawares less receptive to his ministrations, Brainerd wrote in frustration, "The manner of their living is likewise a great disadvantage to
the design of their being Christianized. They are almost continually
roving from place to place."[16] Despite his frustrations, Brainerd's
persistence, coupled with the threat of removal, converted perhaps
a dozen Delawares who were still living near the present site of Nazareth, including Tatamy and his family.

Unsurprisingly, Brainerd's account of Tatamy's conversion is ge-
nerically Calvinist. In Brainerd's view, during late July 1744, while he
preached and the knowledgeable but spiritually slumbering Delaware interpreted, Tatamy "was somewhat awaken'd to a concern for
his Soul; so that the next Day he discours'd freely with me about
his spiritual concerns, and gave me an Opportunity to use further
Endeavours to fasten the Impressions of his perishing State upon his
Mind." Still "these impressions seem'd quickly to decline, and he
remain'd in a great Measure careless and secure, until some time
late in the Fall of the Year." For several weeks Tatamy languished.
"At this Season divine Truth took hold of him, and made deep Impressions upon his Mind. He was brought under great Concern for
his Soul, and his Exercise was not now transient and unsteady, but
constant and abiding, so that his Mind was burden'd from Day to
Day, and 'twas his great Enquiry, *What he should do to be saved.*"[17]

According to Brainerd, Tatamy lost considerable sleep and was
"under a great Pressure of Mind . . . while he was striving for Mercy."
Then, paraphrasing Tatamy, Brainerd tells us that "there seem'd to
be an impassible Mountain before him. He was pressing towards

Heaven as he thought, but his Way was hedg'd up with Thorns that
he could not stir an Inch further. He look'd this Way and that Way,
but could find no Way at all." Tatamy labored persistently but in
vain for deliverance. He could not "help himself thro' this insup-
portable Difficulty." Then, "he says, he gave over striving, and felt
that it was a gone Case with him, as to his own Power, and that all this
Attempts were, and forever would be vain and fruitless." Brainerd
applied the introspective skills for which he is renowned to Tatamy's
case, trying to discern whether "his own *Imagination*" or "divine *Illu-
mination*" was at work. He was "satisfi'd 'twas not the meer Working
of his Imagination" when Tatamy became "divorc'd from a Dependence upon his own Righteousness, and good Deeds."[18] Brainerd's
account goes on in considerable detail to chart the change in Tatamy. He seemed "as if he was now awaked out of Sleep." He became convicted of sin and misery. He sensed the "impossibility of
helping himself by any Thing he could do" and after giving up all
hope of saving himself had a powerful mental impression assuring
him of hope. Brainerd continued with painstaking attention to Tatamy's transformed identity:

> He can't remember distinctly any Views he had of Christ, or give any
> clear Account of his Soul's Acceptance of him, which makes his Experi-
> ence appear the more doubtful, and renders it less satisfactory to himself
> and others, than (perhaps) it might be if he could remember distinctly
> the Apprehensions and actings of his Mind at this Season.
>
> But these Exercises of Soul were attended and follow'd with a very
> Great Change in the Man, so that it might justly be said, he was become
> *another Man*, if not a *new Man*. His Conversation and Deportment were
> much alter'd, and even the careless World could not but admire what
> had befallen him to make so great a Change in his Temper, Discourse,
> and Behaviour.

Brainerd saw in Tatamy's "publick Performances" external evidence
of his changed nature. Now he preached with "admirable Fervency,
and scarce knew when to leave off." This change was "*abiding*,"
Brainerd noted, so much that Tatamy was no longer tempted,
though "much expos'd to *strong Drink* . . . moving free as Water; and
yet has never, as I know of, discover'd any hankering Desire after
it." Finally, when Tatamy manifested "considerable Experience of
spiritual Exercise, and discourses *feelingly* of the Conflicts and Con-
solations of a *real* Christian," Brainerd was satisfied.

The whole process made Tatamy appear "like another Man to his

Neighbors."[19] A baptismal ceremony on July 21, 1745, ritually symbolized the changing cultural identities of Tatamy and his wife, whose name is unknown. Tunda Tatamy became Moses Tatamy. Similarly, Joseph Peepys, Thomas Store, Isaac Still, John Pumpshire, and Stephen Calvin exchanged traditional names for appellations of apostles, or, in Calvin's case, Brainerd's favorite Reformer. These were the same Delawares who stayed in the Forks or New Jersey and adapted to English property ways.

Pennsylvanians who were not as critical of these Delaware conversions as Richard Peters saw in them metamorphosis from the hardening categories of "savage" to "civilized Indian." If these Pennsylvanians never quite considered Tatamy one of them, at least the propertied Presbyterian was on his way to becoming "one of our Indian Friends."[20] By the 1750s Tatamy thought of his property as "my place in the forks," and even temporary relocation was noteworthy.[21] He had learned to write, as had his son William. His daughter, Jemima, enjoyed "the advantage of some schooling."[22] The Land Office agent who filed Tatamy's 1733 application noted that "Tattemy an Indian has improv'd a piece of Land . . . he is known to Wm Allen . . . he desires a Grant for the said Land."[23] Allen endorsed Tatamy's request. By "improving" and acquiring recognizably English rights to property, and finally by fully embracing Presbyterianism, Tatamy identified himself in loose terms as a peer of fellow Presbyterian and property holder William Allen. If the remaining socioeconomic gulf mocked such tenuous parity, still Tatamy's cultural adaptations gained him a degree of acceptance in eighteenth-century Pennsylvania society that most Delawares never achieved. Both Tatamy and Allen left their name on the modern Lehigh Valley landscape.

Tatamy's choices were not those of most Delawares, however. Brainerd's account laments the "paganism" he believed beset the Susquehanna Delawares and their Native American neighbors. He could not reach them as he did Tatamy. But many of these were attracted to the Moravians, including Teedyuscung, who remained on the fringes of the Walking Purchase for several years. The Iroquois deeded to Pennsylvania the land lying north of the Walking Purchase in 1749. Simultaneously, Teedyuscung and other Delawares living in kinship groups at Meniolagomekah received baptism at the nearby Moravian mission, christened *Gnadenhutten* (huts of grace), at present Lehighton on the western edge of the Walking Purchase. The Moravians apparently attracted Teedyuscung's half brother,

Weshichagechive, because Moravian Indians "were very happy & contented in their Hearts, & that they liv'd no longer like other Indians, doing bad Things."[24] He requested baptism and was designated Nicodemus in June 1749.

Members of Weshichagechive's kinship followed, as the Moravians hoped they would, including Teedyuscung, whose conversion process is less known than Tatamy's but no less significant. As Brainerd did, the Moravian missionaries sought signs of true change in Teedyuscung but found him "unstable" and of a "wavering disposition." Apparently Teedyuscung was deeply moved by the doctrine of redemption from sin through Christ, however. He became "convicted of sin" and lamented that he was forbidden a baptismal ceremony. After passing cleanly through a probationary period, "he was baptized in the little turreted chapter on the Mahoning" River. The Moravian bishop who performed the ceremony noted on March 12, 1750, "Today I baptized Tatiuskundt, the chief among sinners."[25] Jane Merritt assessed the rationale of Teedyuscung and his kin. "Perhaps" they converted "to combat the dissolution of their family and community, perhaps to use the connections of the Moravians with other whites to strengthen their claims on land at the Forks of the Delaware, and perhaps to express what they felt in their hearts."[26] Perhaps they were moved by some combination of all these. Wallace thought so, but for the nineteenth-century Moravian chronicler Reichel, the matter was less nuanced.[27]

Waxing romantic in his rehearsal of Teedyuscung's conversion, Reichel juxtaposed Christian, "civilized Indians" with "savage" ones, lamenting that neither a Christian name nor "solemn ritual" was sufficient to transform a "savage" into a "Christian":

> The ceremony was performed in accordance with the solemn ritual observed among the Brethren at that time in the baptism of adults; and when the straight-limbed Delaware, robed, in white, rose from bended knee, he rose as Gideon. . . . Thus Teedyuscung became a member of the Christian Church, and yet failed, as so many do, to become a Christian. The lessons of the Divine Master whom he had promised to follow proved distasteful to him, as he found they demanded renunciation of self, the practice of humility, the forgiveness of injuries, and the return of good for evil. They were different from the doctrines taught in the school of Nature in which he had long been educated.[28]

Though Teedyuscung's longings were undoubtedly heartfelt, and his wife and other family members joined him in converting, Reich-

el alluded that Teedyuscung was not content to settle down, as Tatamy had promised to do, in "enjoyment of the same Religion &
Laws with" European settlers. So, in Reichel's ironic wording, Teedyuscung "resisted the influence of the Good Spirit that sought to
dispossess him of the resentment that burned within his soul when
he remembered how his countrymen were being injured by the
whites, and how they had been traduced and were being oppressed
by the imperious Iroquois."[29]

Neither Reichel nor Wallace has fully explained the forces that
pulled Teedyuscung in opposing directions. He was emotionally
scarred by Canassatego's assault on Nutimus, to whom Teedyuscung
was kin, and to whose status as sachem Teedyuscung became heir.
In 1750 Nutimus traveled from Nescopeck on the Susquehanna,
where he had settled with Delawares Brainerd thought irredeemable
pagans, to proselytize Teedyuscung "back to the old Indian way."
Details are unclear, but apparently Nutimus suspected the Moravians were only more agents of dispossession, come to take not only
land but all else that was sacred.[30] Teedyuscung apparently adopted
that view and tried to persuade his kin and other Delaware converts
to leave the mission.[31]

Teedyuscung moved north to the Wyoming Valley in the spring
of 1754. Displaced and highly dissatisfied, he and other Delawares
brooded over "the Injuries they had receiv'd from the English in
being cheated of the Fork Lands and obliged to retire farther back
over the Mountains[.] This so enraged them that they resolved no
longer to bear the Injuries."[32]

Braddock's July 9, 1755, defeat by the French and allied Indians
gave Delawares "a favourable Opportunity of taking Revenge" for
the injustices of the Walking Purchase.[33] Delawares and allied Shawnees gained confidence and lost regard for British soldiers on the
same day. They "prepared for war," Reichel wrote, by rehearsing the
injustices they had suffered, "chiefly," he thought, "the fraud of
1737, perpetrated, as they maintained, to confirm the deedless purchase of all that tract of country which extended from the Tohickon
and the Hills of Lechauweki northward and westward." Delawares
determined that "wherever the white man was settled within this disputed territory" they would attack by surprise and without mercy—
taking scalps and prisoners, burning homes, outbuildings, and crops.
"The frontier," wrote A. D. Chidsey, "was about to reap the harvest
from the seeds of discontent sown by the Proprietaries and the Pro-

vincial authorities."[34] The Moravian chronicler Reichel called this "savage warfare," distinguishing it from the civilized style.[35]

Delawares and allied Shawnees descended on the outskirts of the Walking Purchase and decimated settlers. Easton, Bethlehem, Nazareth, and the hinterland became a hotbed of fear and activity as outlying settlers were killed, scalped, burned, and kidnapped with horrifying stealth and efficiency. On October 16, 1755, Delaware warriors descended on settlers at Penn's Creek below Shamokin, killing thirteen and capturing as many more. Beginning October 31 Scots-Irish settlers were visited with several days of raids. At Great Cove on the Susquehanna half of the ninety-three settlers were captured or killed. By early November settlers were aware of a second Delaware war party, which ranged from the Tulpehocken Valley to the Minisink and over the Delaware River into New Jersey, ever nearer the heart of their former homeland. On November 24 they struck and burned Gnadenhutten, the Moravian settlement on Mahoning Creek and the edge of the Walking Purchase. Eleven victims "were scalped, or shot, or tomahawked, or burned to death, the prelude only had been performed to the tragedy which the savages were resolved to enact within the precincts of the by them detested walking–purchase."[36]

On December 10 Delawares killed Frederick Hoeth and his family and destroyed the home, the barn, and the mill they had imposed on the landscape. This systematic horror continued family by family—Everhart, Hartman, Culver, McMichael, Marshall, Broadhead, Hauser—and rapidly southeastward toward the heart of the Walking Purchase. Led by Teedyuscung, the Delawares returned to the Forks for vengeance. Richard Peters, reporting the terror to Thomas Penn, penned this biographical sketch: Teedyuscung "was born among the English somewhere near Trenton," Peters wrote,

> Is near 50 Years Old, a lusty, rawboned Man, haughty and very desirous of respect and Command. He can drink three quarts or a Gallon of Rum a day without being drunk. He was the Man that persuaded the Delawares to go over to the French and then to Attack the Frontiers. He commanded the attacks at Gnadenhutten and he and these with him have been concerned in the Mischiefs done to the Inhabitants of Northampton County.[37]

Teedyuscung remembered "the indignities that had been heaped upon him and his kinsmen of the Forks by the imperious Canassa-

tego, at the Treaty of 1742."[38] He returned to assert his masculinity
and take what he regarded as rightfully his. His leadership poses
challenges for those inclined to see Delaware feminization as negotiated, willing subservience.

Teedyuscung's Delawares and allied Shawnees took more than
one hundred lives in and around Northampton County in just a few
months. Most poignantly, on November 24, 1755, they attacked the
Moravian settlement on the east side of the Mahoning adjacent to
Gnadenhutten and slew or captured several men, women, and children. Reichel's pathetic narrative of the massacre makes vivid for his
readers a version of the capture of Susannah Nitschmann and the
burning of Anna Sensemann and Gottlieb and Johannah Anders,
cradling an infant. A few Moravian eyewitnesses escaped to relate
the awful tale, but George Fabricius was not among them. "He was
pierced simultaneously by two balls and fell. Rushing upon him the
infuriated savages buried their tomahawks in his body and scalped
him down to the eyes. Next day his mangled corpse was found in a
pool of blood on the spot where he had been butchered."[39]

Bishop Spangenburg wrote words of comfort to his Delaware Valley flock after the massacre. His language was conciliatory, at least
compared with that of non-Moravian settlers in the Forks who vowed
to repay Delaware aggression in kind. But Spangenburg repeatedly
labeled Delawares and their allies the "barbarous enemy," "savages," and "devils." The Moravians were as Job, tried and afflicted,
but could take comfort that an overseeing God controlled their
fates, and "if He will have us safe, not all the devils will be able to
hurt us in the least. What could Satan do to Job, to his children,
and to his cattle and his horses, before he was permitted by God?"[40]
Spangenburg ended his message by appealing to his hearers to pray

> that the Lord may rebuke the wicked Prince of Darkness who is the great
> leader of these idolaters that are now crying against Christ's people; and
> that He may fill these poor ignorant wicked creatures with fear and
> trembling, and thus cause them to return to their hills and mountains
> as the proper companions of wolves and bears, and other wild beasts, till
> the Lord please to open their eyes and to call them from the power of
> Satan into his glorious kingdom.[41]

Ironically, the Delawares intended all along to "return to their hills
and mountains" and threatened their kinsmen who remained loyal
to the Moravians that their ears would be opened with a hot iron

if they refused to heed the call.[42] But by 1755 Moravians considered the Forks rightfully theirs. To qualify as "civilized Indians," Delawares had to make the same concession and adopt confessional Christianity. Scotch-Irish settlers were generally unwilling even to negotiate that far. "They professed to believe that the Indians were the Cananites of the Western World," and therefore subject to a divine extermination order. The Moravians' Delaware converts "were murdered whenever an opportunity presented itself." Partly conscious of the irony of his words, local historian William Heller realized, "The Moravians experienced less difficulty in taming these savages than the government did in subduing the Scotch-Irish, who, discovering the weakness of the government, formed themselves into lawless, armed bands, murdering the Indians wherever they were to be found."[43]

Delawares flooded the Moravian settlements, seeking protection from the arbitrary violence.[44] The Moravians petitioned the Pennsylvania government to protect loyal Delawares against the aggressors. A November 29, 1755, letter dictated by fourteen Indians, including five Delawares, among whom was a Moravian named Augustus, pleaded with Governor Morris to protect them. They specifically cited conversion and recognition of English property ways as justification. "We have hitherto been poor heathen," the petition said, but "the Brethren have told us words from Jesus Christ our God and Lord, who became a man for us and purchased salvation for us with his blood." They believed and credited the Brethren who had "permitted us to live upon their land." This acknowledgment of the efficacy of Christianity and legitimacy of Moravian land rights under Pennsylvania law earned these Native Americans the protection of the colony. "As you have made it your own choice [to] become members of our civil society, and subjects of the same Government, and determine to share the same fate with us," Governor Morris replied to their petition, "I shall make it my care to extend the same protection to you as to the other subjects of his Majesty."[45]

For Delawares, membership in "civil society" required acknowledgment that the land belonged to colonists. Tatamy and loyal Moravian converts—those covered by the designation "civilized Indians"—met that requirement. Teedyuscung and other "savage warriors" did not. Pennsylvanians developed nomenclature freighted with racial and theological implications to make sense of the violence. Delawares unwilling to adapt attacked with "fiendish ferocity." They were therefore "savages" and "demons."[46] The upheaval in the wake of the Walking Purchase caused all Delawares to make hard decisions about who they were and how they would live. The majority opted for something between Tatamy's course to civilized Indian and Teedyuscung's path to savage devil. Reporting to the governor in 1757, Moravian Matthew Schropp wrote, "Indians residing here in Bethlehem on one hand are not inclined to settle again in the Indian country for fear of their lives, and on the other cannot resolve to live below Philadelphia for want of hunting opportunity."[47] Perhaps Reichel had these in mind when he conceived of some of the Indians near Bethlehem as "half civilized."[48]

Delaware retribution took an especially high toll on Edward Marshall, the only walker to finish the day-and-a-half walk in 1737. Marshall felt the proprietors had been stingy with land patents after he performed the walk that defined the purchase. He swore that the Delawares had been ill treated. He had no affection for Delawares, however, and they none for him. When violence broke out he took his family to New Jersey and remained until spring 1756. In apparent acts of reciprocity, Delawares descended on his home near Jacobus Creek, shot his daughter Catherine and kidnapped his pregnant wife, whose scalped remains were later discovered in the Pocono mountains. Having not found Edward at home, Delawares returned in August and killed his son, Peter, but again missed their main target.[49] Their skulking way of war made dehumanizing the enemy easier for Europeans, who feared desperately "those barbarous savage Indians."[50] European settlers imagined that "from their lurking places in the fastnesses of the Great Swamp, the savage warriors, led by their king in person, would sally forth on their marauds, striking consternation into the hearts of defenseless settlers, ruthlessly destroying with torch and tomahawk, and then retreating."[51] Meanwhile, Marshall acquired the heroic reputation of an adroit Indian hunter, making it hard to distinguish "savage" skulkers and scalpers from "civilized" ones except by race. Woods lore has Marshall taking revenge on Indians for their ferocious attacks on his family. He is supposed to have said that when he met an Indian he shut one eye and they never met again. He is legendary for outfoxing Indians in the woods by coaxing them into the open, where he quickly ended their lives.[52] George La Bar, a descendant of early French settlers north of the Forks, liked to kill Delawares as well as Marshall did, or at least he told his children so. "Squads of men might often be seen, with George as their captain, looking for 'game.'" Tom Casper also enjoyed a reputation as "a great Indian-slayer," and a German resident of Hunter's settlement "used to boast that he had killed fourteen without getting a scratch."[53]

Clearly an insatiable demand for land led to the imposition of anthropological categories informed by tenuous racial and religious justifications. Otherwise there is no discernible difference between the violence enacted by Delawares and by European settlers. And one need not rely on folklore alone to illustrate how Pennsylvanians constructed rationales for violent dispossession of Delawares.

On December 16, 1755, Edward Shippen wrote to the Pennsylvania chief justice William Allen, foremost holder of Forks real estate, informing Allen of a "courageous, resolute" frontiersman curious to "know whether any handsome premiums is offered for scalps, because if there is he is sure his force will soon be augmented."[54] Weeks later Richard Peters wrote to Thomas Penn to assure him that no matter how much he spent to defend the colony, "little good will be done without giving handsome rewards for scalps." Peters reported that Governor Morris and the Provincial Council were sure of the "necessity" for scalp bounties. A potential problem, as Peters saw it, might come of indiscriminate scalpers doing violence to Delawares "who are or may be inclined to be our friends."[55] Three days later Peters wrote to Penn again, assuring him that "since the encouragement proposed to be given for scalping and the Governor and Commissioner's tour amongst the people in the back counties, their spirits seem to revive." Already several companies of frontiersmen had "voluntarily offered themselves" to take advantage of cash for scalps.[56]

Conrad Weiser wrote to Thomas Penn, observing that

rudeness, lawlessness, and ignorance of the back inhabitants . . . will bring a general Indian war over us. They curse and dam the Indians and call them murdering dogs into their faces without discrimination, when on the other hand these poor Indians that are still our friends do not know where to go for safety; in the woods they are in danger of being killed, or their young men joining our enemy. Among us they are in danger of being killed by the mob.[57]

Delawares were indeed caught in an awful dilemma. They could have no sense of security or independence among the Iroquois, the Pennsylvanians, and the French. From the Wyoming Valley in November 1755 the Delawares Weiser had in mind sent word to Governor Morris, emphasizing their dependence on and loyalty to the

English, begging for information and assurance. "We are as children here," the message read, "till we receive words. We believe that we are in great Danger For we hear the Hatchets fly about our Ears and we Know not what will befall us, and therefore We are afraid."[58] The anxiety was similar among settlers. Richard Peters wrote to Thomas Penn that "almost all the women and children, over the Susquehanna, have left their habitations and the roads are full of starved, naked, indigent multitudes, who but the other day lived with comfort and satisfaction."[59]

In Philadelphia on April 14, 1756, Governor Robert Hunter Morris declared war on the Delawares over the opposition of a Quaker-dominated assembly. Sir William Johnson, King George's deputy for Indian affairs in the northern colonies, who was just then planning how he could conciliate Delawares through Iroquois diplomatic channels, fumed that "these hostile Measures which Mr. Morris has Entered into is Throwing all our Schemes into Confusion" and giving the French an advantage. "What will the Delaware & Shawonese think of Such Opposition and Contradiction in our Conduct?"[60] Meanwhile Thomas Penn wondered about a rather different French advantage stemming from contradictory English conduct. Reflecting that scalp bounties would lead to "private murder" of men, women, and children, Penn expressed his concern that "in some of the French pieces lately published we are reproached with it as a cruel and unchristian-like practice."[61] Apparently, though Penn relied on the benchmark of French standards to gauge his civility, French critics found it difficult to discern between savage and civilized scalping.

The anxieties born of settling and civilizing the woods spurred the development of overt civilizing influences. A jail was among the first buildings constructed at Easton, in 1753. Soon it was full of convicted horse thieves—nine from 1752 to 1755. In 1754 Easton's citizens petitioned the trustees of a fund raised to establish schools in the colonies. William Parsons, Easton's leading citizen, wrote to Richard Peters that the Eastoners "are so perverse and quarrelsome in all their affairs that I am sometimes ready to query with myself whether it be man or beast that the generous benefactors are about to civilize." He added, "It seems to me like attempting to wash a Blackamoor white."[62]

It helped psychologically in this process of civilizing Northampton County to have "beasts" and "Blackamoors" against which one could contrast. Delawares served this purpose. As Jane Merritt demonstrated, "Racial rhetoric displaced the nuances of the negotiated interactions that had previously characterized relations between white settlers and native Americans."[63]

The tumultuous social and cultural transformations and adaptations that rocked the Upper Delaware River valley in the wake of the Walking Purchase defied all attempts at categorization. English and German settlers sought to impose "civilization" in the same way they imposed lines on the landscape. Just as the lines were often arbitrary and subjective, so were the cultural identities into which Delawares were fitted despite complicating factors. Neither Christian names nor solemn rituals could always transform Delawares into satisfactorily civilized Christians after the English or Moravian fashion. But neither could surveys, maps, or official deeds easily transform Lenapehoking into baronies and manors. Both Delawares and Pennsylvanians responded to the dissonance violently, Delawares to regain a lost voice and a vanishing landscape; Pennsylvanians, to quiet that voice and recast the landscape. The violence only evoked more dissonance.

8

Appearing Fair and Just

And as for you who are likely to be concerned in the government of Pennsylvania . . . I do charge you before the Lord God and his only angels that you be lowly, diligent, and tender; fearing God, loving the people, and hating covetousness. Let justice have its impartial course. . . . use no tricks, fly to no devices to support or cover injustice.

—William Penn to My dear Wife and Children,
Warminghurst, 4 August 1682.

. . . the Indians being utterly unacquainted with Reading and Writing, keep no Records of their Sales of Land, or other Transactions; and that therefore their Knowledge of what their Ancestors did, being only traditional, is imperfect, and often very erroneous: A most glaring Instance whereof appears in the present Complainants against the Proprietaries in their Ignorance (if it is real) with respect to the Purchase made of their Ancestors by the old Proprietor, Mr. Penn, of the Land in and near the Forks of Delaware, to which they now pretend to set up this Claim, tho' it was actually and fairly sold by the Indian owners thereof so long ago as the year 1686 as we expect fully to make appear to your Honour. . . . all the Proprietaries Indian Purchases appearing fair and just . . .

Report of the Committee of the Council,
Historical Society of Pennyslvania.

PROPRIETARY POLICIES FOR HANDLING COMPLAINTS ABOUT THE WALKING Purchase rendered Delawares powerless through the diplomatic channels forged between them and William Penn and his agents. Displaced and highly dissatisfied, Delawares brooded over "the Injuries they had receiv'd from the English in being cheated of the Fork Lands and obliged to retire farther back over the Mountains[.] This so enraged them that they resolved no longer to bear the Injuries."[1] When Braddock's army was decimated in July 1755, Delawares returned to settlements in the Forks with tomahawks, muskets, and firebrands to seek redress of grievances with the only methods that remained in their power. Very quickly Delawares regained a voice and negotiating leverage. Their attacks ended as suddenly as they had begun when Governor Morris initiated diplomatic ties and invited Teedyuscung to meet him at Easton in July 1756. When Morris later tried to change the meeting location to Bethlehem, Teedyuscung said they would meet at Easton, and they did. The horrifying violence had accomplished its intended purpose. It regained Delawares a semblance of power, a place at the negotiating table.

Seeking to explain the vicious bursts, historians have argued that the Walking Purchase was a relatively minor offense and therefore unable to account for Delaware violence two decades later. They too easily accept official proprietary records that distance the Penns and their agents from blame by locating the cause of Delaware violence entirely within French quarters. These sources and their offspring create an impetuous, drunken, opportunistic Teedyuscung for use as a scapegoat on which to blame Delawares' demands for justice twenty years after the Walking Purchase. Since the sources simultaneously consider Teedyuscung incapable of masterminding Delaware protests of such scale, he is considered the puppet first of the French and then of jealous Quaker manipulators who, having forfeited power in the Pennsylvania assembly but retained the impulse to share in provincial affairs, formed the Friendly Association for Regaining and Preserving Peace with the Indians.

Though proprietorial sources nearly monopolize historical interpretation, Charles Thomson's 1759 *An Enquiry into the Causes of the Alienation of the Delaware and Shawanese Indians,* captured a truer picture. The Walking Purchase, Thomson argued, presaged Pennsylvania's loss of Delaware alliance after Braddock's defeat.[2] Only the oft-repeated memory of benevolent relations nurtured by William Penn in the 1680s, combined with a Delaware sense of powerlessness in the face of European settlement and the Pennsylvania-Iroquois alliance, persuaded the Delawares to postpone retaliation. Just as soon as the French afforded them "a favourable Opportunity of taking Revenge" for the injustices of the Walking Purchase, the Delawares capitalized.[3]

In early 1756 as Pennsylvania declared war on Delawares and Sir William Johnson planned to subdue them diplomatically, a series of meetings occurred in Philadelphia between Delawares and weighty Quakers. These councils spawned cooperative efforts to achieve peace by demanding accountability from the proprietors for the injustices of the Walking Purchase.[4] Financing this movement were members of the Friendly Association.[5] The innocuous name of the group belied its influence, and what the proprietors and their agents considered its meddlesome intrusion into proprietary affairs. The Friendly Association worked with the Pennsylvania Assembly to investigate Delaware claims. It sent representatives and food to treaties and negotiations and provided substantial amounts of goods to satisfy Delaware claims. Clearly the association also sought to discredit the proprietary party, but historians relying on proprietary accounts have overstated this motive as a determinant of the association's benevolent if also self-interested diplomacy.[6] The Friendly Association came under the leadership of Philadelphia merchant Israel Pemberton, whose grandfather, Phineas, arrived in Pennsylvania on the *Welcome* with William Penn in 1682. More than seventy years later, the descendants of William Penn and Phineas Pemberton battled over Penn's conflicted legacy and the future of Pennsylvania.

The Penn heirs secured the loyalty of the Provincial Council and agents in their employ. Pemberton found allies among Quakers on both sides of the Atlantic, Moravians and Mennonites, Delawares led by Teedyuscung, Senecas of the Iroquois Confederacy, and antiproprietary assemblymen led by Benjamin Franklin. Both the proprietary party and the antiproprietary coalition would argue their case before the king's Privy Council, which remanded it to the Board of Trade, which would order Sir William Johnson to hear the case. While orders went back and forth across the Atlantic, the fight over the Walking Purchase took many turns.

In late summer 1756, newly appointed lieutenant governor, William Denny, ignorant of Walking Purchase details and naïve of the proprietors' previous handling of accusations of fraud and deception, received word from Delawares at Tioga that they would meet with provincial officials at Easton, conditioned on the attendance of their Quaker allies. Funded largely by the Friendly Association, the conference began on November 8, 1756.

Teedyuscung informed the lieutenant governor that the "Abundance of Confusion, Disorder and Distraction" between the Pennsylvania government and his people was the result of the social and cultural upheaval they had experienced but assured him that they were reorganized and that he was authorized to transact public business. As Denny and his commissioners treated with Teedyuscung, it became apparent that the Delaware king was implying that "Injustice had been done them in Land Affairs."[8] Privately "a warm debate arose between the commissioners and Provincial Secretary Richard Peters, the proprietors' chief informer and confidant, about what should be said to the Indians." Some thought Teedyuscung ought to be asked directly about the cause of Delaware aggression. Peters urged the governor to avoid such questioning since it was obvious that the French had incited the Delawares. "The Commissioners, however, declared that the question had never been asked the Indians officially, and Secretary Peters finally consented, that they might be asked in a general way, why they were dissatisfied; but that no direct query as to whether the Proprietaries or their agents had wronged them would be allowed." Israel Pemberton thought Peters conspired to hide the truth.[9]

When Pennsylvania and Delaware officials next met on November 12, 1756, Denny inquired, "Have we, the Governor, or People of Pennsylvania, done you any Kind of Injury? If you think we have, you should be honest, and tell us your Hearts: You should have made Complaints before you struck us, for so it was agreed in our antient League. However, now the great Spirit has thus happily brought us once more together, speak your Mind plainly on this Head, and tell us if you have any just Cause of Complaint." The Delawares were delighted by such frankness, according to Pemberton, and Teedyuscung asked for the rest of the day to consider his answer. It was agreed that he would speak plainly of the matter the next day.[10]

On November 13, 1756, at the Easton conference, Teedyuscung outlined the Delaware case against the proprietors regarding the Walking Purchase. The injustice done the Delawares was not the sole cause of their late hostilities, he said, but "the Cause why this Blow came harder upon you than it would have otherwise done."[11] The soil on which he then stood, he said, "was his Land and Inheritance, and was taken from him by fraud."[12] When asked what, precisely, he meant by fraud, Teedyuscung charged the sons of William Penn with forging the 1686 document and using it to "take Land from the Indians which they never sold."[13] Asked to explain himself, Teedyuscung reaffirmed that all land from "Tohiccon over the great Mountain to Wyomink has been taken from me by Fraud; for when I agreed to sell the Land to the old Proprietary by the Course of the River, the young Proprietaries came and got it run out by a straight Line by the Compass and by that means took in double the Quantity intended to be sold."[14] In the aftermath, Teedyuscung charged, the Delawares had been molested by settlers who objected to Delaware hunting and gathering—in other words, to a continuation of Delaware culture on the landscape.

These charges repeated and enhanced old Delaware concerns with the Walking Purchase. They acknowledged that an agreement, reached in or about 1686, specified that land along the Delaware as far as a man could walk in a day and a half was to be measured and paid for by the proprietors. The line was to follow the Delaware River northward, however, not tack northwest as it did "by the Compass." "Instead of beginning at Wright's Town and going back into the woods a north westerly course, as they did, they [walkers] should have gone along by the courses of the River Delaware or the nearest Path to it." Moreover, the Delaware argued, "they walked too fast and should not have kept walking constantly, but have frequently stopp'd to smoak a pipe." The fact that they did not meant "that the Length of the Walk was unreasonable and extravagant."[15]

Teedyuscung added a charge that Manawkeyhicon had marked the 1737 quitclaim illegitimately, he having no claim to Forks lands. In this way "the Proprietaries, greedy to purchase Lands, buy of one King what belongs to the other." These substantial charges stung secretary Peters and the Provincial Council, who assumed a defensive posture. Lieutenant Governor Denny asked Peters and Conrad Weiser their respective views on Teedyuscing's charges. Each remembered the affair as James Logan had constructed it between 1735 and 1742. Weiser said that, "as to the Lands particularly instanced by Teedyuscung, he heard they were sold to, and the Consideration Money paid by, the first Proprietary, William Penn.—That when Mr. John Penn and Mr. Thomas Penn were here, a Meeting was then had, with the principal Indians living on these Lands, and the former Agreement renewed, and the Limits again settled between the Proprietaries and those Chiefs of the Delawares, and accordingly a Line was soon after run by Indians and Surveyors. That the Delawares complaining afterwards, their Complaint was heard in a great Council of the Six Nations, held at Philadelphia, in the year 1743 [1742]." Weiser was careful to avoid implicating the proprietors. Moreover he deflected the charge, as they had done, by arguing that none of the Indians present had any interest in the land anyway. Richard Peters assured the governor of Weiser's account, adding, "When the Matter should come to be well examined into, the Proprietaries would not be found to have done Injustice to the Delawares." Peters's outward certainty was betrayed by the zealous manner in which he personally prevented the matter from ever being fairly investigated.[16]

Denny assured the Delawares that he would have the matter "thoroughly enquired into, and if it should appear that Injustice had been done the Delaware in this, or any other of their Sales, they ought to receive Satisfaction." The commissioners encouraged Denny to back away from this promise and use the extra goods supplied for the treaty by the Friendly Association to "offer them immediate Satisfaction." The next day Denny attempted to conciliate the Delaware with presents. Teedyuscung refused to accept the gifts as compensation for the injustices of the Walking Purchase, citing the fact that many whose claims to the land had been violated were not in attendance. He promised to bring them with him to Easton for another conference the following spring.

Provincial Secretary Richard Peters took the official minutes for the conference and was careful to shield the proprietors. Having adamantly refused to record the meat of Teedyuscung's charges, he worried that Charles Thomson, a clerk Denny appointed at Teedyuscung's request, had been too exact in his minutes. Peters visited trustees of the Friendly Association in their boardinghouse on November 15, 1756, and demanded to see Thomson's minutes. He was sure they included Teedyuscung's charges that the proprietors had purchased the land from those who had no claim on it. "Mr. Franklin's interpretation, to blacken the Proprietors and support a party," Peters called it and expurgated such slander from the official record. Instead he negotiated the difficulty by explaining that the walk itself was a disgrace, to be sure, but that the proprietors were innocent bystanders who "always despised it" and would not have been party to it except that they had "paid several times for" the land within its bounds.[17]

In Philadelphia after the Easton conference, Franklin, Joseph Fox, John Hughes, and William Masters—assemblymen appointed as commissioners to the treaty—filed a report criticizing the official minutes. "The Warmth and Earnestness" of Teedyuscung's charges were "too faintly expressed." They desired it noted that whatever made it into the official record from Weiser's and Peters's "palliating Heresay Accounts of the Walking Purchase," all in attendance acknowledged the injustice of the affair. No objection had been raised when Teedyuscung emphatically asserted fraud. Secretary Peters himself had been heard to characterize the Walking Purchase as "unworthy of any Government," and he privately wrote to

Thomas Penn that the Delaware used "Express terms" when attributing the severity of their hostility to the Walking Purchase.[18]

Teedyuscung's "express" accusations justified the existence of the Friendly Association and fired their commitment. They organized themselves officially with the primary goal of financing further treaties to create peace in the province—and to facilitate the prosecution of Teedyuscung's case. Initially Lieutenant Governor Denny was pleased to have the association's wealth at his disposal. He sent word to Teedyuscung that he would be compensated for the fraud if he could present a compelling case when they next met at Easton.[19] Meanwhile Denny facilitated the Friendly Association's efforts to copy deeds related to the Walking Purchase.[20]

Increasingly concerned at these developments, Richard Peters immediately recognized that Teedyuscung's charges had the potential to change public opinion, that blame for the hostilities could be shifted from the pacifist Quakers to the apparently rapacious proprietors.[21] He sent a copy of the treaty minutes to Thomas Penn in England with an excited letter, in which he worried that the Friendly Association's antiproprietary rhetoric was infecting Teedyuscung, and that the Quakers had unlimited resources with which to buy the loyalty of the Delaware king.[22] Penn sent back post haste, ordering Peters to employ Conrad Weiser to mollify Teedyuscung.[23] He also wrote to Denny, ordering him to stop allowing the Quakers "to concern themselves in any treaty with the Indians, or on any pretense to suffer presents from such persons to be given to the Indians." Thereafter Denny forbade the Friendly Association to treat in any official capacity, or as a group, with the Delawares.[24] Meanwhile secretary Peters stalled the Friendly Association's effort to collect the documents needed to make a case for proprietary malfeasance in the Walking Purchase by denying Pemberton direct access to the records.[25]

Denny met Teedyuscung and a large retinue of Delawares during the last week of July 1757 at Easton, where they renewed the negotiations of the previous fall. After ceremonial rites Teedyuscung spoke, asking the lieutenant governor to "look with all Diligence, and see from whence our Differences have sprung. You may easily see they have sprung from the Land or Earth." Teedyuscung implored Denny to use his power to look into the Walking Purchase documents and "do what may be consistent with Justice." Denny asked the Delaware interpreter, John Pumpshire, to clarify Teedyuscung's meaning; Pumpshire explained, "The Land is the Cause of our Differences, that is, our being unhappily turned out of the Land, is the cause." Hostilities could have been prevented, Pumpshire added, if the proprietors had given the Delawares an alternative place at which to settle.

The records show the proprietary agents still "confused" by Tee-dyuscung, perhaps owing to the king's reportedly frequent inebriation during conference speeches. However, Teedyuscung's crystal clarity regarding Walking Purchase issues, combined with selective hearing and recasting by the proprietary agents, suggests that their confusion may well have been feigned. Denny sent Provincial Secretary Richard Peters instructions to meet with Teedyuscung and "consider well the Speeches the King had made, and afterwards explain them to me." When Teedyuscung clarified his meaning for Secretary Peters, he made confusion hard to fake. "The Complaints I made last Fall, I yet continue," Teedyuscung said. He then rehearsed his charges:

> I think some Lands have been bought by the Proprietary, or his Agents, from Indians who had not a right to sell, and to whom the Lands did not belong. I think also when some Lands have been sold to the Proprietary by Indians who had a Right to sell to a certain Place, whether that Purchase was to be measured by Miles or Hours Walk, that the Proprietaries have, contrary to Agreement or Bargain, taken in more Lands than they ought to have done, and Lands that belonged to others. I therefore now desire that you will produce the Writings and Deeds by which you hold the Land, and let them be read in publick and examined, that it may be fully known from what Indians you have bought the Lands you hold, and how far your Purchases extend, that Copies of the Whole may be laid before King George, and published.[26]

Teedyuscung promised to make no demands about any land fairly purchased, but "If the Proprietors have taken in more Lands than they bought of true Owners, I expect . . . to be paid for that." The Delaware king assured Peters that his people did not presume to displace settlers who had encroached on their lands but would peacefully settle in the Wyoming Valley provided they could get "certain Boundaries fixed between you and us; and a certain Tract of Land fixed, which it shall not be lawful for us or our Children ever to sell, nor for you or any of your Children, ever to buy."[27]

With these points clarified, in their next meeting Denny explained to Teedyuscung that although he had intended to fulfill his

promise and satisfy Delaware charges of injustice, the Walking Purchase had gone before the king's ministers,

> who, looking upon it as a Matter of great Importance, determined that
> it should be carefully enquired into, and examined, before some Person
> no ways concerned in Interest, on whose Honesty and Judgment they
> could depend; and therefore appointed Sir William Johnson to hear the
> Particulars of your Charge, and the Proprietary's Defense, and lay the
> whole Mater before His Majesty for his Royal Determination, in order
> that he may do you Justice himself, if you are injured.[28]

Teedyuscung refused to go meet with Johnson in New York. He knew
of Sir William's reputation for fairness toward the Iroquois, but this
caused concern rather than hope. Teedyuscung was "sensible that
some of the Nations are there that have been instrumental to this
Misunderstanding." The Iroquois had, Teedyuscung remembered,
"called us Women and threatened to take us by the Foretop, and
throw us aside as Women." Teedyuscung had too bitter memories
and too much pride to go to Albany and risk subjecting himself to
the abuse he watched Nutimus suffer at Canassatego's hands in
1742. He would, he said, assent to Johnson's deputy George Croghan's investigating the case if he would provide relevant deeds and
other documents to Johnson and the king. "I want nothing but to
see the Deeds fairly looked into," Teedyuscung said, "and true Copies of them taken, and put with these Minutes now taken," and he
wanted it done by "a Clerk of my own."[29]

Conceding Teedyuscung's demands, Denny urged the Delaware
king to agree to peace and not wait for the Walking Purchase to be
settled. These were "trifling Considerations" compared to peace,
Denny reasoned; "let us therefore for the present suspend them."
Some of the Delawares agreed and urged Teedyuscung to "settle the
peace, and let all these Disputes stand till after." Teedyuscung was
inclined to listen to them, but he demanded as a condition that he
have copies of the relevant deeds and letters from the king, his ministers, and the proprietors, and that private conversations between
him and Denny "be entered with these Minutes, and that it may be
read in publick at our next Meeting."[30]

Avoiding the Friendly Association, Conrad Weiser met with Teedyuscung privately early on August 2, 1757, to ask the leading question
"whether he wanted to see all the Deeds of the Province from the
first Purchases, or only those relating to the Back Lands where we

are?" Weiser explained that he asked the question because only deeds relevant to Teedyuscung's complaints had been taken to Easton. "Teedyuscung answered, I should be well pleased to have seen all the Deeds, as the Country to the Sea Shore was first ours; but if there be the Deeds for these Back Lands, which is the Main Point, I will be contented, so that I see them, and have Copies of them, and of the Letters from the Kings Ministers or Proprietaries; as soon as that is done, I will not say one Word more about the Differences or Lands, but confirm the Peace." Two days later, on August 4, 1757, Denny assured Teedyuscung that Charles Thomson had seen and copied the relevant deeds. The official minutes say that Thomson told Teedyuscung that he had indeed made copies of the copy of the 1686 document, the 1737 quitclaim, and the two October 1736 documents drafted by James Logan and signed by the Iroquois, releasing all claims the Six Nations had to land along the Delaware, but Thomson's own version of these events is not clear on that point. Apparently Teedyuscung felt confident that he finally had faithful reproductions of the relevant documents. He exacted Denny's promise that copies would be sent to King George II.[31]

The enduring Easton conference of the summer of 1757 neared its peaceful end. Diplomatic details remained, however. For the conference to end properly, Denny noted, Teedyuscung must yield the prisoners held by the Delawares. Teedyuscung chafed at the belated nature of this request but finally assured Denny, "Whatever shall be in our Power, we shall endeavor to do." Then, adding his own last request, Teedyuscung told Denny, "You must deliver me my just Due about Lands."[32] A final wampum belt was exchanged; presents were given to the Delawares, followed by feasting, reaffirmation of the peace, "and a Variety of Indian Dances." Two days more of negotiating details followed. Teedyuscung gained Denny's promise that Thomson would not be hindered from copying deeds and the treaty minutes or sending them to King George II under the auspices of Isaac Norris and the provincial assembly. He added, now that the Delaware and English were allied in war against the French, his warriors would expect to be paid as English soldiers were, and that they would not be subject to English officers. "We understand our own way of fighting better than you," Teedyuscung explained, thus bringing to conclusion a treaty in which he had aired his complaints regarding the Walking Purchase and negotiated for a settlement based on true copies of the relevant documents.[33]

The results of Teedyuscung's impressive negotiating, however,

were diminished by his naivete. He assumed too easily that he would
be given the relevant documents, and that they would hold the key
to justice's being done in King George's council or Sir William Johnson's court. Teedyuscung and the Delawares did not need anyone to
tell them to complain about the Walking Purchase, but they were
necessarily dependent on a political and legal culture in which they
were strangers. They were at the mercy of merciless men who, rather
than disclose and clarify, were inclined to conceal and confuse.

Back in Philadelphia a committee of provincial councilors investigated and reported on the charges Teedyuscung made in 1756 and
renewed in July and August 1757. The two Quaker committeemen,
Benjamin Shoemaker and William Logan, dissented when it became
apparent that the remaining five members perceived their role to
be disputing, rather than investigating and discerning the accuracy
of, Teedyuscung's charges. This coincided with Thomas Penn's view
of the committee's role. He wrote to Governor James Hamilton that
William Logan, by airing his views on the injustice of the Walking
Purchase, "has not acted a fair part in his professions to me."[34] The
five partisans of the proprietors filed a lengthy, detailed, and ex-
traordinarily legalistic report on November 24, 1757.[35] Its orienta-
tion became baldly apparent in its first sentence, which announced
that the committee had investigated "Agreeable to the Order of
Council, appointing us a Committee to enquire into the pretended
Causes assigned by the Indians at the said Treaty for their striking
the English, and destroying so many of our back Inhabitants, and
their Complaints of Injustice said to be done them by the Proprietaries in some of their Indian Purchases."[36]

The committee chided the credulous Delawares for supposing
that the Walking Purchase "should only be an idle trifling Walk such
as a Person would take who had little else in View but to spend the
Time in Pleasure, killing game and every now and then sitting down
to smoak his pipe." Instead they drew attention to the precise language of the 1737 quitclaim, arguing that it "was not to be such a
walk, but read Day and Half's *Journey*," so, technically, "the Walkers
were not strictly to be confined to Walking."[37]

"Perhaps it may be objected," the commissioners conceded, "that
Mr. Eastburn took more Liberty in his Map than he was warranted
to do by the said Deeds for that Purchase." But "to obviate and answer which objection" the committee composed a stunning combination of survey data and legal terms, evoked precedents from other
(irrelevant) purchases in which lines went west rather than north,

and by the end persuaded themselves if no one else that "it necessarily follows that the Course of the said Walk and of the South Westerly Line of this disputed Purchase, from the utmost Extent of the most Westerly Branch of Neshaminy . . . must be North Westerly as Mr. Eastburn has laid it down in his map." From there it was not a great leap to justify the survey line bearing northeast toward New York. "We cannot but think, as Mr. Eastburn did, that it is most rational and equitable that the said Head or Cross Line should run at Right Angles from the Course of the Walk." The Delawares might have wondered why such a self-evident fact was not included in the terms of the quitclaim? Moreover, how could such a survey be construed, as it was in the committee's report, as "without favouring one Side or the other"?[38]

Of all Teedyuscung's charges, the committee struggled most with the alleged forgery of the 1686 document, of which, as in the 1730s, only a copy could be produced. The committee asserted that Thomas Holme had, at absentee William Penn's request, negotiated with the Delawares in 1686. Since they could not produce a deed proving the outcome of these negotiations, the committee assembled "other corroborating Circumstances and Proofs, particularly some Entries in an antient Diary of William Markham . . . which mention the said Mr. Markham and Captain Holme's treating with the said Delaware Indians for the Purchase of the said Lands in the Forks just before the Date of the said Deed of the 28th August 1686." This evidence only showed that negotiations had been conducted, with perhaps as much as a preliminary agreement being drafted, but no proof of payment made or final agreement reached. Still the committee cast their data as proof of a binding purchase of vaguely specified land. "Besides," they argued, had not the "Delaware Indians themselves" implied the authenticity of the 1686 document when they signed the 1737 quitclaim, thereby authorizing the walk stipulated in 1686? This bit of obfuscation was silent about the misleading map and assurances that the walk would not end in eviction from the Forks, both of which were preconditions of the 1737 quitclaim. Ultimately the committee's report simply asserted that the copy of the 1686 document was authentic and countercharged "malicious suggestions and Management of some wicked People, Enemies to the Proprietaries, who had come to the Knowledge of that Circumstance of the said Deed's being lost, and that there was nothing but a Copy of it now to be found which they would have it believed was a forged one." These thinly veiled references to "busy

forward People" turned, by the end of the report, to open condem-
nation of the "Majority of the Assembly at the Time when the
House, from their unhappy religious Principles or from what other
Motive they best knew, refused or declined to concur with the Governor in giving the Hatchet to and joining with those Indians against
the Enemy." In this way the committee's report to the governor deflected each of Teedyuscung's charges as "imaginary Reasons for
their Quarrel with us" and located the actual source of the conflict
with French incursion and hypocritical Quakers too fastidious to
fight but quite adept at stirring up war. Cast this way, the official proprietorial interpretation obtained in the mind of many Pennsylvanians but was challenged again at Easton in June 1762.

On August 29, 1759, King George issued an official Order in
Council authorizing Sir William Johnson, his deputy of Indian affairs in the northern colonies, to hear the Delaware and proprietary
cases and reply with relevant data and his best judgment of how the
matter ought to be settled. Johnson was no particular friend of the
Pennsylvania proprietors or their cause but was clearly biased toward
Britain generally and jealous of his authority in America. "I am the
only person appointed to hear your Complaint," he reminded Delawares on June 23, 1762. Johnson arrived at Easton with long-standing contempt for the Friendly Association's methods of regaining
peace. An intercepted letter piqued his ire. Drafted June 14, 1762,
by Witham Marsh, the assembly's secretary for Indian affairs, the letter encouraged Teedyuscung not to keep his appointment with
Johnson at Easton, but wait "to meet him when all the Indians are
together." Teedyuscung's son showed the letter to Johnson, who
noted that Joseph Fox, a Friendly Association Quaker, had paid ten
pounds for a horse to carry the messenger to Teedyuscung.[39] Such
meddlesome measures are interpreted as evidence of Quaker methods designed "to *prevent* a settlement of Teedyuscung's charges,"
but this is a misreading of Friendly Association interference.[40] Pemberton, Fox, and others in the Friendly Association accurately
viewed themselves as leaders of the few colonists with genuine interest in a just settlement of Teedyuscung's claims. Clearly they were
willing to meddle to accomplish that design and competition between proprietary and assembly parties fueled them, but the idea
that Quakers wanted to *prevent* a just and peaceful settlement of the
Walking Purchase cannot be supported. Even so, Johnson went to
Easton in June 1762 convinced that Quakers were causing Teedyuscung's dilatory behavior.

Johnson and Teedyuscung began the conference on June 18 with the usual ceremonial cleansing and reconciliation. Johnson assured the king of both his authority and his will to see justice done and recommended that Teedyuscung "keep Sober during the Meeting." Teedyuscung assured Johnson that he would be given the same status among the Delawares that he had in Iroquoia. Then, before adjourning, Johnson ordered Richard Peters to read aloud the commission he and Benjamin Chew had been given to act on behalf of the proprietors.[41]

On Saturday, June 19, 1762, Johnson began by thanking Teedyuscung for past goodwill at similar meetings. Teedyuscung replied in kind by apologizing for the rashness of his French-inspired young men and by freeing a young captive woman. Teedyuscung then requested, "I want a Clerk to take down what I may have occasion to say." Johnson, pointing to his secretary, said, "Here is the secretary appointed by the King," explaining how "unprecedented" any other arrangement would be. "Yet Teedyuscung persisted some time to have a Clerk, on Account of his Grandchildren, who ought to have something to shew in writing as well as the English." Here for the first time Johnson either misunderstood or disregarded Teedyuscung's wishes for written records that could be evoked authoritatively in future meetings. Instead he told his secretary to read his minutes aloud so auditors could vouch for their accuracy.

Either satisfied or forlorn, Teedyuscung recalled his relations with Johnson for the past two years, noting their earlier agreement that Teedyuscung could access relevant deeds with which to make the case that he had been defrauded of his homeland. "Where do these Lands lye? Let them be described," Johnson replied. Teedyuscung answered: "The Lands I complain about lye from this Place up the river Delaware to Samuel Dupuy's at the Gap, to the Kittatinny Hills, or blue Mountains, and along the Top of those Mountains to Allimingey; from thence to Mackcungee, from thence to Shammony and from thence across to Delaware River at Pitcock's Creek, and from thence to Easton.[42] Continuing, Teedyuscung explained,

Some years ago, Newtymas, (then Chief of the Delawares) made some Complaint to Mr. James Logan, now deceas'd, who told Newtymas, it wou'd not be worth his while to trouble himself about the Lands: "if you do said He, you'll make the big Trees and Logs, and great Rocks and Stones tumble down into our Road"; and added, He did not value Newtymas, but look'd upon Him as the little finger of his left Hand; but that

He himself was a great, big man; at the same time Stretching out his
Arms.

When Nutimus had complained that the deeds must be wrong,
Logan assured there was no chance of that, "For if any one writes
any thing out of his own Head, We hang him." At Easton in 1762
Teedyuscung demanded that "somebody must have wrote wrong,
and that makes the land all bloody."

What lands did Logan mean?, Johnson wondered. "The same
Lands as above described," Teedyuscung replied. Johnson asked if
what Teedyuscung had called the "Breach occasion'd by Mr. Logan's Words" was the sum of his complaints. Not to be dismissed so
casually, Teedyuscung implored Johnson to "consider of what He
had Said; and when He had Consider'd, to bring out the Deeds."
Teedyuscung had witnessed Logan's dramatic gestures and tones at
Pennsbury in 1736 and again at Philadelphia in 1742. He had listened to Nutimus in the wake of those meetings and remembered
how crucial the deeds were to the initial dispossession of his people.
The meeting adjourned with Johnson's assurance that he would
look into the charges. Another meeting was appointed for Monday
morning, at which time the proprietary commissioners were to be
"ready to answer the Charge relative to the Lands."[43]

Monday morning, June 21, 1762, Teedyuscung and Johnson met
again with their respective retinues, including several members of
the Friendly Association, who sat quietly for the time being. They
listened for about four hours as Richard Peters and Benjamin Chew
read back a history of the Walking Purchase in terms of the Provincial Council's official 1757 report, "also several Deeds, original Letters, Affidavits, Affirmations, and other papers were read openly in
the Hearing, and in the presence of Teedyuscung, and a great Number of Auditors, both Whites, and Indians." According to minutes
in Johnson's papers, Teedyuscung and the other Delawares were satisfied with the proprietary case, "for they very well understood the
purport, or meaning of what had been read."[44]

When the parties met the next day Johnson invited Teedyuscung
to "establish your Right to the Lands in dispute, or object to what
had been said yesterday." Johnson advised Teedyuscung to have his
answer recorded and then "publickly read" to prevent the mistakes
Teedyuscung suspected had darkened previous meetings and
caused this whole "breach occasioned by Mr. Logan's words."[45]
Johnson also invited Teedyuscung, accompanied by two counselors

of his choosing, to inspect the deeds supplied by the proprietary commissioners. Teedyuscung responded by handing Johnson a note in which he assured that neither he nor the other Indians had understood any of what had been said or the writings presented the previous day. He again demanded his own clerk and insinuated that Johnson, commissioned by the king to do justice, was faring no better than Croghan had earlier. Johnson simmered then boiled as he read the short message from Teedyuscung and eight of his Delaware associates. It read:

> Brother Johnson;
> You promis'd to see Justice done, but when you refus'd to let me have a Clerk, I began to Fear you intended to do as George Croghan did, when We were here five years Since. King George has order'd you to hear me, and all the Indians fully. But how do you think I can make Answer at once to as many Papers as *your Clerk* was four Hours reading, in a Language I do not understand, and which have not been interpreted to me? I expect to have all those Papers deliver'd to me, that I may have time to Consider them, and if you refuse this, I, and all the Indians shall see you do not intend to do Justice, and we shall Complain to King George, who We are Sure is our Friend. . . . We know the King will do us Justice.[46]

Convinced that Teedyuscung could not have conceived such thoughts himself, Johnson badgered the king to reveal "who put it in his head." Teedyuscung claimed the sentiments originated in "his own Heart, and was the Sentiment of all his people." Then he tried to mollify the heated Johnson by saying he had not meant to imply that Johnson would act unjustly, but too late. Johnson was offended and reacted by coloring Teedyuscung as ambivalent, as issuing an accusative statement and then withdrawing the accusation, as saying one day he understood the proprietor's case and swearing the next day that he did not. Johnson's characterization of Teedyuscung resounds as the prevalent theme in Wallace's biography of the Delaware king. However, Friendly Association members challenged Johnson's profile of Teedyuscung as the negotiations unfolded.[47]

Johnson made his point about Teedyuscung's ambivalence by assuring the king that a cloud of witnesses could confirm that he had expressed his satisfaction with and understanding of the prior proceedings. No sooner had this attack on Teedyuscung's supposed mind change left Johnson's lips than Israel Pemberton rose and shot back.

Since Sir William had appeal'd to the By-Standers for the Truth of this matter, He thought Himself oblig'd to declare, that Teedyuscung said no such thing, and that the Minutes were not fairly taken: that many material Things which Teedyuscung had said, were altogether omitted, and other Things misrepresented: that it was unreasonable, to call on Teedyuscung to answer a number of Title Deeds and Proofs, produced yesterday on the part of the Proprietaries, which took up three Hours and an half in reading, especially as they were wrote in English, not one Sentence of which Teedyuscung understood.[48]

Johnson warmly quizzed Pemberton why he presumed to speak, reminding all present and perhaps reinforcing his own conviction that "He was, by the Royal Order, to hear the Complaints of the Indians, and the Proprietaries Defence, and that no other person had any right to Intermeddle." The proprietary commissioners sitting by, who must have been heartened by this spectacle, became even more so when Johnson exemplified their respectful decorum, implying strongly that Pemberton should do likewise. Instead Pemberton lashed back, asserting his right and obligation as a freeman to see justice done and threatening that Teedyuscung would have his own clerk or complaints would reach King George's court, where justice would be done.[49]

Bickering over whom, precisely, the clerk served, Johnson or the king, quickly gave way to the core issues when Johnson observed that "He plainly saw thro what Channel Teedyuscung conducted his Business." Here Joseph Fox, especially meddlesome in Johnson's eyes, chimed in: "Teedyuscung did not understand a word of what was read yesterday, nor did He say, that He understood it." Joseph Galloway announced that he had been sent by the assembly to see justice done and the welfare of Pennsylvania protected and wondered why Johnson had not responded to the assembly's petition for a written copy of the proprietor's claim to the Walking Purchase. Johnson answered that he would first make his report to King George before letting the proceedings become public. When challenged on that point, Johnson demanded that his antagonists hush: "that matters would go on quietly, and He wou'd do Justice, if they would let Business go on in its proper Channel, and desired they wou'd not interpose; for He wou'd not Suffer, or put up with such Treatment." Pemberton retorted with his threat to circumvent Johnson, who again ordered silence to no avail. He rose and ordered his translator to tell Teedyuscung that the conference would stand adjourned.[50]

Until that moment Teedyuscung and the Delawares were conspicuously absent from this narrative. With other accounts, including Friendly Association minutes meager and incomplete, we cannot know what role if any Delawares played in this outburst, or exactly what relationship they shared with their Quaker defenders. It is desirable but impossible to know what Teedyuscung thought of what was happening before his eyes.

As Johnson left the bench Benjamin Chew got him to clarify that, since Teedyuscung announced that he did not understand, the deeds would be shown him again and interpreted to his satisfaction. Quakers, meanwhile, offered documents in defense of Teedyuscung's case as Johnson muttered something about not doing business in a mob. Back at his quarters, Johnson dictated a letter assuring the Delawares that he would meet with them to hear their complaints and show them "such Deeds and Papers as you may judge proper." Only let there be no "busy people interfering in this matter," Johnson warned, reiterating, "I am the only Person appointed to hear your Complaint, and to Send it to the Great King."[51] It took a day for Montour to find Teedyuscung and deliver the message, after which Captain Bull, a son of Teedyuscung, delivered Johnson a request from the king for an evening meeting.

On June 24, 1762, Teedyuscung captured his hearers' attention when he capitulated: "I deliver up the Lands to you." He then gave Johnson copies of two deeds, including the 1718 conveyance in which Sassoonan transferred rights to land below the Lehigh Hills and between the Delaware and Susquehanna rivers to the proprietors. Probably coached by Charles Thomson on this point, Teedyuscung offered this document as evidence that in 1718 the proprietors assumed no claim to the lands they would later take by virtue of the supposed 1686 deed. Teedyuscung fully understood and intended to communicate contempt for the repeated but hollow promise that he could have access to documents that would substantiate his complaints. If Johnson would do no better than the Pennsylvania governor at providing deeds, Teedyuscung would. Giving Johnson a letter drafted by his cousin and interpreted by Isaac Still, Teedyuscung restated the injustices done the Delawares in the Walking Purchase and the inherent injustices of Johnson's court. The letter also carefully capitulated, offered to sign a release and "bury under Ground all Controversies about Land."[52] To his credit, Johnson ordered it read. The letter clarified that Teedyuscung had spoken to Johnson of his own mind, "without the knowledge and advice of any white

man." Nutimus, he said, was his source, both of authority among the
Delawares and of resentment of the Walking Purchase. The letter
then rehearsed the events of the Walking Purchase, allowing that an
agreement for land had been made with William Penn and the land
measured by a walk ending in what Teedyuscung called Conshohop-
pen, in present Bucks County. Then in 1718 the agreement with Sassoonan was made, fixing the Lehigh Hills as a northern boundary.
Nutimus sold Logan the Durham tract nearly a decade later. Then,
according to Teedyuscung's own memory, "about seven years afterwards, Neutimus, and some other Indians, were invited to meet the
two young Proprietors at Durham. I was then there; and in the next
Spring they met again at Pennsbury, where a paper was shewn to
Neutimus, and other Chief men who were there, which they were
told was the Deed our Fathers had Signed, but They knew it was not,
and therefore said so; upon which they were threaten'd in the manner I told you before" by James Logan. Teedyuscung emphasized,
"I was there present, and heard it with my own Ears." Apparently
unaware of Logan's alliance with the Iroquois, Teedyuscung knew
that Delaware sachems had been pressured by the Iroquois to sign
the quitclaim of 1737. That fall men "walk'd over the Forks of Delaware, up beyond the . . . Mountains, by the course of a Compass,
different from what was ever intended; and thus They took away our
Lands." When the Delawares threatened to drive back the waves of
settlers and complained to the Bucks County justice of the peace
Jeremiah Langhorne, a conference was called for Philadelphia in
1742. There James Logan displayed the 1686 document as authentic. "Tho it was not," according to Teedyuscung's memory, "the
Minquas believ'd them, and telling us We were women, they took
us by the Hair of the Head," referring to Canassatago's assault on
Nutimus, "and removed Us off the Land."[53]

Having restated the events of the Walking Purchase in terms more
passionate and clear than any previous recorded statement, Teedyuscung curiously chose this opportunity to concede the authenticity
of the 1686 document. "It now appears by sundry old Writings and
Papers, which have been shewn by the Proprietary Commissioners,
and read at this Conference, that the said Charge of Forgery, was a
Mistake; into which Mistake, we were led by the Accounts We had
receiv'd from our Ancestors concerning the Land sold by Mayhker-
rick-ksiho, Sayhoppey, and Taugh-haughsy, to old William Penn, in
the year 1686." He maintained that the walk itself was unfairly per-

formed but allowed that "difference in opinion may happen without either of Us being bad men."[54]

With that retraction, the twenty-five-year feud over the Walking Purchase effectively ended. Teedyuscung offered to sign a release for the lands in question. Knowing such a document would impugn the claim the proprietors asserted all along, Governor Hamilton persuaded Teedyuscung that a new quitclaim would be extraneous. Sir William Johnson accounted to the lords of trade with his understanding of what had happened, shaping forever the way the Walking Purchase and Teedyuscung would be understood. Reporting on August 1, 1762, to the lords of trade regarding the Walking Purchase hearing, Johnson noted (on the basis of affidavits of men with interest in Walking Purchase lands) that "Teedyuscung was stimulated to these Jealousies & instigated to this behavior" by Israel Pemberton and the Friendly Association.[55] Johnson stated further, "Teedyuscung himself hath since declared to me, that he never should have troubled the Proprietors about these lands had he not been instigated to do so by the Quakers."[56]

Johnson's papers include no record of Teedyuscung's ever making such a statement, though the Delaware king is documented to have said otherwise. Speaking to Johnson at Easton on June 24, 1762, Teedyuscung reviewed, "When I spoke to you five days since I knew there was some part of the Land I claimed which the Proprietors had a Deed for, but I thought it best to make them say all they could about the Lands above Neshaminey. This I can assure you I did without the Knowledge and advice of any Whiteman. Nutimus told me so when he gave me his place of chief man among the Delawares."[57] Isaac Still, the Delaware interpreter, attested that Teedyuscung had conceived of the demands he made of Johnson—to see the original deeds and have the services of the clerk of his choice— "without any white person whatever being present or consulted with about it."[58]

Still some historians have seen Johnson's report as powerful evidence of Teedyuscung as Pemberton's pawn, a pliable weapon in a fight between Pennsylvania's assembly allied with out-of-office Friendly Association members against the proprietors.[59] This view prefers Johnson's filtered version of events to Teedyuscung's own words. And it fails to account for Teedyuscung's skillful and firm negotiation with Johnson in the exchanges between them in June 1762. Rather than a conspiracy in which Teedyuscung simply fronted for the Quaker faction, the culmination of the Walking Purchase debate in 1762 was a triumph of British imperial power over Delawares unequipped to negotiate the complexities of the colonial systems that obtained. Clearly Teedyuscung was aided and even coached by Quakers and Charles Thomson, but the evidence cannot support the old notion that Teedyuscung's charges were no more than fabricated attempts by unempowered Quakers to spite the proprietor and his council.[60] Nor can it be substantiated, as Ralph Ketchum argued, that "Quaker success in publicizing charges of proprietary land fraud" occurred as "hapless Indians" were "deviously and cynically manipulated" by selfish Quakers.[61] Despite the colorful June 21 outburst, Teedyuscung and Johnson dominated the meetings. Both spoke angrily and Teedyuscung eloquently as he outlined for a final time the injustices of the Walking Purchase. He ultimately conceded the proprietors' case not because he had only been passively asserting a Quaker cause, but because he was wearied—"almost tired" in his words—and concluded that there would be no redress.

Johnson sympathized with Teedyuscung's position somewhat when he made recommendations to the lords of trade. Concluding his report, Johnson wrote:

> Thus my Lords this dispute is at length brought to a Conclusion—The Indians appear satisfied that the Charge of fraud and forgery ascribed to the Proprietaries is a mistake, and nothing seems to remain of the truth and fairness of which the Indians do not acknowledge except the Walk of a Day and an half, and as they for the sake of peace & friendship have nevertheless give up that point, and as the Proprietaries have obtained this tract of Land for a trifling consideration in respect of the worth of the Lands, and this Tribe of Indians being very poor, I would beg leave to recommend that the Proprietors make them a handsome present as a Token of their friendship for them, and this I conceive will make them effectually easy under this their concession.[62]

The summer conference in 1762 ended quietly then, a briefly contentious but ultimately uneventful denouement to an episode that capped the transformation of Lenapehoking into Pennsylvania, and that saw Penn's Woods' transition from a religious experiment by which William Penn hoped to manipulate land, populate his colony, and thereby gain wealth by a policy of peaceful possession of Delaware lands to a secularized real estate enterprise in which Penn's sons and their agents hoped to achieve the same ends peacefully or otherwise. They lacked the bridling influence of a theology that fostered humanism and kindled a sense of accountability, but they fully inherited a colonial mentality and notions of landscapes that could be possessed. Against this momentum Teedyuscung and the other Delawares had little power. He asked one last request. "I desire to let you know something about some New Englanders," Teedyuscung said to Johnson on June 28, 1762. They "are coming to Wyoming. . . . neither I, nor my people will stop them; but as you are in authority, I desire you'll endeavor to prevent their coming, as they may breed mischief between us and them." Johnson promised to do his best. Pennsylvania governor Hamilton said he would write to General Amherst and the governor of New England. Teedyuscung promised not to fight the encroachment. Before a year passed the New Englanders had burned him to death.

9

Dimensions of Delaware
Power in Penn's Woods

Whatever shall be in our Power, we shall endeavor to do.
—Teedyuscung, in Julian Boyd,
Indian Treaties Printed by Benjamin Franklin

A MARBLE FRIEZE IN THE ROTUNDA ATOP THE U.S. CAPITOL DEPICTS DELA-
wares negotiating with William Penn the proverbial Great Treaty of
1682.[1] This is just one of the multitude of ways Americans have "iconocized" the emblematic event.[2] But as the supposed episode does,
the artworks inspire images of a middle ground—a promised land—
that, though imagined, never materialized in any sustained way.

Penn's initial description of his "tract of land in America" as "altogether Indian" did not account for two generations of Dutch,
Swedish, and some English presence, yet it represented a dramatically different conception from that which obtained in Virginia and
New England, where colonists considered the land *vacuum domicilium*, unoccupied and eager to be subdued.[3] Even so, it may be that
holy experiments are born with the germs of their own declension.[4]
Thomas Gordon argued that William Penn expected his colonists to
exhibit "greater moral and political perfection for his colony than a
just estimate of human nature would warrant."[5] Though Frederick
Tolles and others have emphasized the enduring peace that Penn's
colony enjoyed compared to the rest of British North America,[6] individual interests, including Penn's own, overwhelmed his ideals. His
assumption that Delawares were his legitimate predecessors on the
landscape restrained the powerful idea of possession. Yet the ambiguity inherent in Delawares' inhabiting *Penn's* Woods suggests the
illusory quality of Penn's notion of peaceable possession. When
pushed, Penn knew, and James Logan showed, that possession must
be enforced—that grants, deeds, and treaties notwithstanding, pos-

session could be defined ultimately only by one's ability to dispossess.

The dissonance generated by dispossessing Delawares required Pennsylvanians to rationalize possession. This task required the adaptation and solidifying of anthropological categories that racialized Delawares and rendered them "savage" not because they behaved savagely, but because they were Delawares.

William Penn did not participate in the overt savage-making process. He negotiated with Delawares on ostensibly equal terms, spoke of them admiringly, even acknowledging as facile his notions of civilization when his meetings with Delawares exposed ambiguities of English culture. Yet Penn gained the power to dispossess Delawares on a practical level by acknowledging their prior possession and giving them goods in exchange. Delawares initially shared power with Europeans to gain the advantages of alliance against the Iroquois. By the early eighteenth century, Delaware need for such an alliance, combined with increasing dependence on European goods, circumscribed their sovereignty further. Now Delawares would depend on allies—Penn, the French, the Friendly Association—to preclude becoming completely dispossessed. Thus as Europeans gained power over the landscape, the dimensions of Delaware power shrank, though this development did not occur in strictly linear fashion. With Penn's 1681 acquisition of their land, Delaware power actually increased. Between 1682 and 1736 Delawares inhabited a fragile middle ground. Negotiation was possible. There was peace if no New Jerusalem. By allying with Penn's government, Delawares became insulated from hostile neighbors. Moreover, Delaware alliance with Penn removed the pressure of Dutch and Swedish encroachment. By showing relatively remarkable restraint, Delawares and William Penn gave a holy experiment credibility, even suggesting the possibility "that we may always live together as neighbors and friends" in a "league of peace."[7]

Right away, however, Penn set surveyors to the task of possession and Delawares became more adept at acquiring goods.[8] The idyllic image Penn had for his woods tended toward conflicts. Surveyors and the settlers who followed them threatened Delaware territoriality. By February 1684 Tammany threatened to undermine peaceable possession. "Hindring our peopl to plant & seat upon their lands by war!" Tammany demanded more gifts. Penn, in turn, nearly abandoned the holy experiment, determined to enforce his possession.[9] Though mitigated, this initial conflict foreshadowed. Materialism,

which underscored possession after any fashion, doomed Delawares
who depended on European goods and Penn's covetous heirs. Dissonance plagued the notion of peaceable possession.

The holy experiment failed in the face of demographic and economic demands on human nature that encouraged the Walking
Purchase. In fact, "Pennsylvania's relations with Indians" went
"steadily downhill" after William Penn left for England for the last
time in 1701.[10] When Penn initially visited his tract of land in
America, his willingness to negotiate with Delawares suggested that
his promised land might become a mutually useful middle ground.
But as James Merrell showed, the practical ways Pennsylvanians and
Delawares behaved relative to land transactions illustrate that "men
sharing the rigors of the paths, wearing the same sorts of clothes,
eating from the same pot, puffing on the same pipe, nonetheless did
not shake their different ways of thinking about the landscape."[11]
All Pennsylvania negotiators, from James Logan to "Honest" Conrad Weiser to the less trusty George Croghan, speculated in Delaware land themselves. They intended to possess a piece of Penn's
Woods and were prepared to enforce such possession.

Nutimus confidently brokered Delaware power in the late 1720s
and early 1730s. But by positioning Delawares against the growing
demands of the Penn heirs and James Logan, Nutimus undermined
Delaware alliance with Pennsylvania. The decline of Delaware
power, manifested in vain threats of alliance with Iroquois against
Pennsylvania and talk of violent retribution for the Walking Purchase, became painfully apparent to Nutimus in 1742. Delawares
were surprised to learn that on behalf of Pennsylvania's proprietors,
James Logan and Conrad Weiser had allied with the Iroquois in
1736 preparatory to expelling Delawares. The Walking Purchase in
1737 feigned a legitimate transfer of Delaware land to Pennsylvania.
Protests followed, met by Canassatego's humiliating 1742 eviction
notice. The Onandaga spokesman's feminization of Nutimus
marked the nadir of Delaware power. They were without friends for
the first time since Penn acquired possession of their land in 1681.

Few in numbers, politically decentralized, Delawares remained
powerless until a new alliance presented. They were willing to ally
with the British, but increasingly British imperialism perceived less
need for Delawares. When the British major general Edward Braddock spurned an offer of Delaware alliance in early 1755, western
Delawares turned to the French, who, along with Shawnees and
Upper Mississippi Valley natives, devastated Braddock's army on July

9.[12] Governor Morris rejected a final attempt by Delawares to ally with Pennsylvania in August 1755. "One word of yours will bring the Delawares to join you," an Iroquois mediator told Morris, but no word of "necessary Encouragement" was forthcoming.[13] No sooner did Morris fail to placate alliance-seeking Delawares than they joined the French, an option made more attractive by Braddock's humiliating defeat. Thus Delawares in 1755 gained "a favourable Opportunity of taking Revenge"[14] for "the fraud of 1737, perpetrated, as they maintained, to confirm the deedless purchase of all that tract of country which extended from the Tohickon and the Hills of Lechauweki northward and westward."[15]

Delawares exercised power in acts of desperate struggle to maintain cultural and geographical ground in Pennsylvania. Though politically weak, they had no intention of accepting dispossession without a fight. Teedyuscung led Delawares against settlements in and near the Walking Purchase, asserting power, rejecting the fraudulent land grab, defying the cultural castration Iroquoia asserted by designating Delawares as women. Such violent spasms represented the one form of power remaining in Delaware control. Denied English alliance against Iroquois or Iroquois against English, Delawares brooded until the French provided some encouragement. As it became clear that England would control North America, Delawares finally capitulated, seeking accommodation in the context of British empire.

Historians have overstated the dimensions of Delaware power at these critical junctures. Wallace wrote that in 1762 Teedyuscung "took matters into his own hands, writing a letter to Johnson [and] appointing a meeting at Philadelphia." Johnson replied, whereupon "Teedyuscung wrote to Johnson."[16] These words invite readers to envision Teedyuscung as Franklin, seated thoughtfully at a desk, dipping into his inkwell before writing a few pensive lines to Sir William Johnson. We are asked to imagine Teedyuscung taking control, setting Johnson's agenda. The treaty documents include his mark, no signature. He lacked the power ultimately to take control. He talked to Johnson only through interpreters, negotiators, and mediators whose presence and influence made cross-cultural communication possible but also, often, problematic. "Negotiators," James Merrell demonstrated, "to defuse a volatile situation, might work not to get at the truth but to shade it, to twist it, and sometimes bury it altogether."[17] Outside butchering colonists, Teeduyscung was impotent. He had no power to take matters into his own hands. He depended

upon memory, which, though keen, was precisely the history that
negotiators irretrievably warped in authoritative documents, "not
one Sentence of which Teedyuscung understood."[18] When colonial
officials refused to credit Teedyuscung's version of events, prefer-
ring instead the past created by proprietorial agents, Teedyuscung
could do nothing more than threaten unpersuasively to appeal to
King George.[19]

Even had Pennsylvania granted Teedyuscung's demand for "certain Boundaries fixed between you and us; and a certain Tract of
Land fixed, which it shall not be lawful for us or our Children ever
to sell, nor for you or any of your Children, ever to buy," it was too
late.[20] Artificially imposed boundaries were easy for Pennsylvania to
alter. Similarly, identities were shaped by the powerful. The negotiations between Delawares and William Penn were closing by the mid-
eighteenth century as Pennsylvania's adaptation of the anthropological categories, civilized and savage, neared completion. Now with
little negotiation, white propertied Pennsylvanians determined who
could be "civilized" and who must remain "savage." Delawares were
fractured, empowered only enough to make a painful decision
whether to comply with the conditions upon which one could move
from one identity to the other. "By late 1763," Jane Merritt wrote,
"many Indians, whether voluntarily or under pressure, went to great
lengths to strip themselves of the remnants of savagism."[21] "*Individuals*," Karen Ordahl Kupperman added, "crossed lines and moved
between English and American identities; some may have crossed
permanently, but most entered a state of liminality."[22] One such
Delaware was Moses Tatamy.

His ability to speak English, his willingness to adopt English farming, and his conversion to Presbyterianism empowered him to continue living at the Forks. He continued to serve Pennsylvania as a
negotiator and translator. During the war over the Walking Purchase, Tatamy furnished clear statements of Delaware history and
evidence against the proprietors. He learned, at least by the 1760s,
to write. In 1769 the Pennsylvania Assembly granted the request of
Tatamy's son, Nicholas, for two hundred acres in perpetuity because
of "the Services of his father, an Interpreter, and faithful friend to
this Province."[23] But conversion to Englishness for the Tatamy family was neither seamless nor painless. Tatamy's son William was shot
by a colonist near Bethlehem in July 1757 and lingered a month before dying. Moses (Tunda) himself apparently died in 1762. His
daughter, Jemima, received an education financed by Friendly Asso-

ciation Quakers. Unfortunately she fades from historical records. Nicholas and his family can be tracked in the 1790 and 1800 census, which lists them as white.[24] It was only possible for Delawares to maintain possession of land at the cost of being identifiably Delaware. Nicholas was "Tatamy, an Indian," in 1769, as his father had been in 1737, but his descendants were white enough for census takers in 1790 and 1800.[25]

Still this was perhaps a preferable fate to Teedyuscung's. Relocated to the Wyoming Valley, Teedyuscung's wife, Elisabeth, fell victim in early 1762 to one of many waves of dysentery. For the next year he resisted the encroachment of Connecticut settlers who arrived under the auspices of the Susquehanna Company. Teedyuscung seemed determined not to relive the Walking Purchase but he was weary of resisting, fighting, and complaining. He was burned to death on April 19, 1763, in his Wyoming Valley home by an arsonist likely sponsored by the Susquehanna Company.

As his father, Teedyuscung, had, Captain Bull joined the Moravians but then migrated in and out of the Walking Purchase land and the variety of cultural identities it fostered, including participation in the raids his father led. Captain Bull traded at Fort Augusta and served the colony as a guide and messenger. Then in August 1763 more than one hundred men set out "to destroy some Indian Towns" along the northern reaches of the Lehigh River. Frustrated in their quest, having retreated from Delaware defenses, a group of the soldiers ambushed "three Indians comeing from Bethlehem," captured them, and stole their goods. By one account the victims were shot and scalped.[26]

When a drunken German officer, Jacob Wetterholt, ordered his men to kill Captain Bull's Moravian cousin Zacharias with his wife and child in August 1763, Captain Bull responded as his father had, in the only way that seemed to remain in his power. He led a Delaware party that tortured and slew all the settlers they could catch.[27] They descended on John Stenton's tavern near Bethlehem on October 8, 1763; killed Stenton; and shot Wetterholt "through the body." They proceeded through Allentown, killing, burning, and scalping as they went, and thence to the Wyoming Valley to enact vengeance for Teedyuscung.

Before Iroquois and British soldiers captured him in March 1764, Captain Bull and his followers horrified settlers in one final frenzy of frustrated vengeance. Even so, there was method in the madness of these outbursts, as there had been when Teedyuscung led the

raids in the 1750s. They were calculated to exact specific vengeance—on Stenton, and Wetterholt—just as Teedyuscung's followers repeatedly sought out Edward Marshall and raided the settlers
of the Walking Purchase. A nineteenth-century family historian was
informed more by the constructed notion of "savagism" than by fact
when he wrote, tellingly, "It is well known that, when the Indians
become exasperated through real or imagined injuries, they consider themselves bound to take revenge on their enemies, without
regard to age or sex; it therefore frequently happens that the innocent suffer with the guilty."[28] Heckewelder knew that the Delawares
"murdered by accident an innocent family," but because they mis-
took the house "they meant to attack."[29] There were, by contrast,
frequent cases of white settlers' scalping and killing Delawares and
other helpless, innocent Native Americans. Most famously, just a few
weeks after Captain Bull's raid on Stenton's tavern, about fifty
armed Pennsylvanians butchered Conestogas living in fear in Lancaster. An observer witnessed "the whole of them, men, women, and
children spread about the prison yard, shot, scalped, hacked and cut
to pieces."[30] Whether Captain Bull's raid motivated this massacre is
unclear. There is a clear connection between Captain Wetterholt's
order for his men to kill Captain Bull's cousin and, in turn, Captain
Bull's order for his men to kill Wetterholt.

    The Walking Purchase is the central event in the declension of
the holy experiment undertaken by Delawares and William Penn.
His vision of Pennsylvania was conditioned by a seventeenth-century
Quakerism, which valued prophecies of Daniel and of John the Rev-
elator and looked forward to an imminent millennial day. Penn assumed that God had promised him Pennsylvania so he could create
an exemplary peaceful, tolerant society, for which he would shortly
be held accountable. With these ideas mitigating proprietary interests, Penn's colony avoided some of the self-righteous tendencies of
other colonies that wreaked more havoc on native peoples. No one,
least of all William Penn, would claim that early Pennsylvania was
utopia, but until 1755 it avoided the ethnic violence that plagued its
colonial neighbors. As late as 1698 Gabriel Thomas noted how "the
English and they [Delawares] live very peaceably, by reason the English satisfies them for their Land."[31] That had as much to do with
Delaware negotiating power and demands on Penn as it did on
Penn's idealism, as shown by the negotiations of 1682 and 1686. The
alliance accommodated the peaceful coexistence both Penn and
Delawares needed. Workable agreements assured everyone contin-

ued access to the landscape and its ecosystems.[32] This was Delawares and Penn "incorporating the Other," as Karen Ordahl Kupperman put it. But simultaneously sown seeds, imperceptible except in phrases like "Their lands," "purchased," "possession," or "John Wood's land," led Pennsylvania and then Delawares to a posture of "resisting the Other."[33] William Penn's vision for Pennsylvania dimmed as he, his heirs, and the colonists they recruited proved unwilling to resist the temptations of the boundless landscape. It begged Englishmen to survey, parcel, plow, and plant. But first Pennsylvania must forcibly possess Delaware land.[34]

If, as Thomas Gordon suggested, Quaker "confidence in the inner light and their belief that this was the eschatological era . . . was without historical foundation," at least their hopes for a "new Jerusalem" endowed them for a few years with a humanism that bridled the idea of possession with a need to be peaceable. Pennsylvania turned more slowly than most British colonies to an insatiable demand for "new opportunities for gain, and unlimited land."[35] Penn genuinely expected God to hold him responsible for keeping Delawares passive by paying them for land. The only dissonance Penn's sons experienced stemmed from indebtedness. Later they expressed some discomfort at being denoted savage by the French press but showed less and less regard for Delawares, whom they thought contemptible, impudent, presumptuous, and savage squatters.[36] Their father conceived of his tract of land in America as "altogether Indian."[37] Their surveyors began using the label *vacant land* on plats describing the Lehigh and Upper Delaware river valleys. Pennsylvania's transformed conception in the minds of its proprietors from "altogether Indian" to "vacuum domicilium" portended the end of its promises of peace.

In his 1682 negotiations with Delawares, Penn became genuinely enamored of their sincerity and wits. "I have never seen more natural sagacity, considering them without the help (I was going to say, the spoil) of tradition; and he will deserve the name of wise that outwits them in any treaty about a thing they understand."[38] The alternative, Penn's heirs and their agents understood, was to outwit Delawares by creating misunderstanding. To that end they sent scouting parties, collaborated with witnesses, cemented secret alliances under false pretenses, cunningly employed a deceptive map, obfuscated reports, and forestalled investigation into their duplicity until, by 1762, it became entirely too late to accommodate Delawares anymore. Still, Delawares sought and exercised what power they could command to avoid being completely dispossessed by Pennsylvanians. They did not go passively. Rather they complained, adapted, retreated, and lashed violently back. They converted and accommodated and gave more than ground.

In his 1693 report, Penn noted that "when the purchase was agreed, great promises past between us of kindness and good neighborhood, and that the Indians and the English must live in love, as long as the sun gave light."[39] A more nearly accurate assertion might adapt a Quaker metaphor to suggest that Delawares and Pennsylvanians could have created a promised land, or at least a mutually accommodating middle ground, as long as Pennsylvanians gave light.[40] Such idealism went unheeded, first by Penn and then wholesale by his heirs and their agents and the ever rising tide of settlers they recruited, given historical realities and human nature in the American environment. William Penn's sons quit the promised land. But given the experiences of Native Americans beyond the Delaware River valley, the combination of Delawares seeking alliance for protection against Iroquois, together with an idealistic if inescapably English proprietor, created an unusually peaceful first generation toward possession. The toll of Penn's distinctive policy of peaceable possession was deferred until the 1750s and 1760s.

John Penn, William's grandson, issued a 1764 proclamation regarding Delawares and all others "who in conjunction with them have committed hostilities." He required "all his Majesty's subjects of this Province, to embrace all opportunities of pursuing, taking, killing, and destroying the same and all others concerned in committing hostilities, murders, or ravages upon this Province." He included bounties for prisoners and scalps. Minus that attempt to civilize a savage command, one is struck that the same rationale informed the Delaware aggression that began almost a decade earlier. They abandoned peace to repay broken promises.

Notes

CHAPTER 1. INTRODUCTION

1. Richard White, *The Middle Ground: Indians, Empires, and Republics in the Great Lakes Region, 1650–1815*(New York: Cambridge University Press, 1991). I use *middle ground*, as Richard White defined the concept, not as a utopian promised land but as a place where possibilities exist and negotiations continue.

2. Jean R. Soderlund, ed., *William Penn and the Founding of Pennsylvania* (Philadelphia: University of Pennsylvania Press, 1983), 307–8.

3. Karen Ordahl Kupperman, *Indians and English: Facing Off in Early America* (Ithaca, N.Y.: Cornell University Press, 2000), 174.

4. "Deed from the Delaware Indians," in Soderlund, *William Penn,* 156–62.

5. Eric Hinderaker, *Elusive Empires: Constructing Colonialism in the Ohio Valley, 1673–1800* (Cambridge: Cambridge University Press, 1997), 89–90.

CHAPTER 2. LENAPEHOKING

The quote opening the chapter is found in C. A. Weslager, *The Delaware Indians: A History* (New Brunswick, N.J.: Rutgers University Press, 1972), 80.

1. Ives Goddard, "Delaware," in *Handbook of North American Indians*, vol. 15, Northeast, ed. Bruce G. Trigger (Washington, D.C.: Smithsonian Institution, 1978), 215.

2. Weslager, *Delaware Indians,* 31; John Heckewelder, *History, Manners, and Customs of the Indian Nations Who Once Inhabited Pennsylvania* (Philadelphia: Historical Society of Pennsylvania, 1876), xli.

3. Marshall J. Becker, "Lenape Population at the Time of European Contact: Estimating Native Numbers in the Lower Delaware Valley," *Proceedings of the American Philosophical Society* 133, no. 2 (1989): 117; and "The Lenape and Other 'Delawarean' Peoples at the Time of European Contact: Population Estimates Derived from Archeological and Historical Sources," *The Bulletin* 105 (Spring 1993): 16–25.

4. Heckewelder, *History,* 50–53.

5. Goddard, "Delaware," 213–16.

6. 12 Quoted in John Bierhorst, *Mythology of the Lenape: Guide and Texts* (Tucson: University of Arizona Press, 1995), 30–31.

7. B. B. James and J. F. Jameson, eds., *Journal of Jasper Danckaerts, 1679–1680* (New York: Scribner's, 1913), 77–78.

8. Archer B. Hubert and William N. Schwarze, eds., "David Zeisberger's History

of Northern American Indians," *Ohio Archeological and Historical Quarterly* 19 (1910): 145.

9. *Journal of Nicholas Cresswell, 1774–1777* (New York, 1924), 117, quoted in Weslager, *Delaware Indians*, 87.

10. William W. Newcomb Jr., "The Walum Olam of the Delaware Indians in Perspective," *Texas Journal of Science* 7 (1955): 57–63.

11. Weslager, *Delaware Indians*, 77–97.

12. Ibid., 91.

13. Ibid., 77–97, reviews the archaeological data and one of Heckewelder's ethnographic accounts; see Heckewelder, *History*, for further ethnography.

14. Bierhorst, *Mythology of the Lenape*, passim.

15. Goddard, "Delaware," 214.

16. Becker, "Lenape Population," 113.

17. Thomas J. Sugrue, "The Peopling and Depeopling of Early Pennsylvania: Indians and Colonists, 1680–1720," *Pennsylvania Magazine of History and Biography* 106, no. 1 (January 1992): 10–11.

18. Quoted in William Newcomb Jr., *The Culture and Acculturation of the Delaware Indians*, Anthropological Papers, no. 10 (Ann Arbor: University of Michigan, Museum of Anthropology, 1956), 11.

19. Sugrue, "Peopling," 12–13.

20. Gabriel Thomas, "The History of West New Jersey," in *Narratives of Early Pennsylvania, West New Jersey, and Delaware, 1630–1707,* ed. Albert Cook Myers, 344 (New York: Scribner's, 1912).

21. Becker, "Lenape Population," 112–22.

22. Anthony F. C. Wallace, "Women, Land, and Society: Three Aspects of Aboriginal Delaware Life," *Pennsylvania Archeologist* 17 (1947): 2.

23. Weslager, *Delaware Indians*, 111, 120; William C. MacLeod, "The Family Hunting Territory and Lenape Political Organization," *American Anthropologist* 22 (1922): 463.

24. Sugrue, "Peopling," 10.

CHAPTER 3. POSSESSION LAWFULLY TAKEN

The quote opening the chapter is found in Thomas Yong, "Relation of Captain Thomas Yong, 1634," in Myers, *Narratives of Early Pennsylvania*, 33–49.

1. A. J. Van Laer, trans. and ed., *Documents Relating to New Netherland, 1624–26* (San Marino, Calif.: Huntington Library, 1924), 17.

2. Ibid., 258–59, 266–67.

3. Weslager, *Delaware Indians*, 116.

4. See Lynn Marie Pietak, "Trading with Strangers: Delaware and Munsee Strategies for Integrating European Trade Goods, 1600–1800" (PhD diss. University of Virginia, 1995).

5. Patricia Seed, *Ceremonies of Possession: Europe's Conquest of the New World, 1492–1640* (Cambridge: Cambridge University Press, 1995).

6. David P. De Vries, "Korte Historiael Ende Journaels Aenteyckeninge," in Myers, *Narratives of Early Pennsylvania*, 17.

7. Ibid.; Michael Dean Mackintosh, "New Sweden, Natives, and Nature: En-

counters in the Seventeenth-Century Delaware Valley," in *Friends and Enemies,* ed. Daniel K. Richter and William A. Pencak, 3–17 (State College: Pennsylvania State University Press, 2004).

8. Daniel K. Richter, "War and Culture: The Iroquois Experience," *William & Mary Quarterly,* 40 (1983): 528–59.

9. De Vries, "Korte Historiael Ende Journaels Aenteyckeninge," and Thomas Youg, "Relation of Captain Thomas Yong, 1634," in Myers, *Narratives of Early Pennsylvania,* 17; Weslager, *Delaware Indians,* 99–110.

10. Weslager, *Delaware Indians,* 106. Bierhorst, *Mythology of the Lenape,* 34, 36.

11. Thomas Yong, "Relation of Captain Thomas Yong, 1634," in Myers, *Narratives of Early Pennsylvania,* 33–49.

12. Ibid.

13. Weslager, *Delaware Indians,* 119; Israel Acrelius, "Account of the Swedish Churches in New Sweden," in Myers, *Narratives of Early Pennsylvania,* 59, 72.

14. Ibid., 73.

15. Weslager, *Delaware Indians,* 119.

16. William H. Browne, ed., *Proceedings and Acts of the General Assembly of Maryland,* volume 9 of the *Archives of Maryland* (Baltimore: Maryland Historical Society, 1899), 520.

17. Weslager, *Delaware Indians,* 122.

18. Becker, "Lenape Population at the Time of European Contact," 118.

19. Amandus Johnson, trans., *Instruction for Johan Printz* (Philadelphia, 1930), 117. Myers, *Narratives of Early Pennsylvania,* 103–4.

20. Acrelius, "Account of the Swedish Churches in New Sweden," in Myers, *Narratives of Early Pennsylvania,* 73; Lorraine E. Williams, "Indians and Europeans in the Delaware Valley, 1620–1655," in *New Sweden in America,* ed. Carol E. Hoffecker, 113–20 (Newark: University of Delaware Press, 1995).

21. Francis Jennings worked hard to demonstrate that neither the Delawares nor the Minquas became subservient to the Iroquois during this period. Francis Jennings, *Ambiguous Iroquois Empire* (New York: Norton, 1984), 113–42; the issue is summarized nicely by Karen Ordahl Kupperman, "Scandinavian Colonists Confront the New World," in Hoffecker *New Sweden in America,* 97–98.

22. Yong, "Relation of Captain Thomas Yong, 1634," in Myers, *Narratives of Early Pennsylvania,* 33–49; MacLeod supports the argument that the Minquas and then Iroquois subordinated Delawares in the seventeenth century in "The Family Hunting Territory and Lenape Political Organization," *American Anthropologist* 22 (1922): 448–63.

23. Heckewelder, *History,* 47–70.

24. *Minutes of the Provincial Council of Pennsylvania* (Philadelphia: Jo. Severns & Co., 1852), 2:546, 3:334.

25. *New York Colonial Documents,* 12:493, quoted in Weslager, *Delaware Indians,* 140.

26. "Examination of Indians about a Murder, October 6, 1670," *Minutes of the Exectutive Council of New York,* 2:502, quoted in Jennings, *Ambiguous Iroquois Empire,* 134.

27. William Penn to My Friends, London, October 18, 1681, in Soderlund, *William Penn,* 88.

CHAPTER 4. PEACEABLE POSSESSION

The quote opening the chapter is found in Gabriel Thomas, "The History of West New Jersey," in Myers, *Narratives of Early Pennsylvania*, 341.

1. Richard S. Dunn, "William Penn's Odyssey: From Child of Light to Absentee Landlord," in *Public Duty and Private Conscience in Seventeenth Century England*, ed. John Morrill, Paul Slack, and Daniel Woolf, 305–23 (Oxford: Clarendon Press, 1993).

2. David S. Lovejoy, *Religious Enthusiasm in the New World: Heresy to Revolution* (Cambridge, Mass.: Harvard University Press, 1985), 116.

3. William W. Comfort, "William Penn's Religious Background," *Pennsylvania Magazine of History and Biography* 68, no. 4 (October 1944): 341–58.

4. Soderlund, *William Penn*, 17–50.

5. Mary K. Geiter, "The Restoration Crisis and the Launching of Pennsylvania, 1679–1681" *English Historical Review* 112(1997): 318.

6. Evan Haefali, "The Holy Experiment of Quaker Colonialism," in "The Creation of American Religious Pluralism: Churches, Colonialism, and Conquest in the Mid-Atlantic, 1628–1688" (PhD diss., Princeton University, 2000), 295–327.

7. William Penn to James Harrison, August 25, 1681, in Soderlund, *William Penn*, 77.

8. J. William Frost, " 'Wear the Sword as Long as Thou Canst': William Penn in Myth and History" (lecture presented at Pennsbury Manor, September 25, 1998), 16–17. Hackneyed references to Penn's holy experiment have largely sapped this reference of its religious significance. Benjamin Trueblood made the holy experiment the motif of his 1894 speech at the placement of a Penn statue atop Philadelphia's City Hall. Ever since, Quaker devotional writers, Pennsylvania government building artists, and Edwin Bronner's highly regarded *William Penn's Holy Experiment* (1962) have secularized the term, fitting it to later American ideals Penn shared while deemphasizing the millennial significance Penn intended. See Benjamin F. Trueblood, *William Penn's Experiment in Civil Government* (Boston: American Peace Society, 1895); Violet Oakley, *The Holy Experiment: A Message to the World from Pennsylvania* (Philadelphia: privately printed, 1922); Maxwell Burt, *Philadelphia: Holy Experiment* (Garden City, N.Y.: Doubleday, 1945); Edwin Bronner, *William Penn's Holy Experiment* (New York: Temple University Press, 1962); Paul Cromwell, "The Holy Experiment" (PhD diss., Florida State University, 1986), Robert Grant Crist, ed., *Penn's Example to the Nations: 300 Years of the Holy Experiment* (Harrisburg, Pa.: Council of Churches for the Pennsylvania Religious Tercentenary Committee, 1987); J. J. Brown, *A Holy Experiment II* (Scottsdale, Ariz.: Visionary Press, 1995); William Kashautus III, *The Making of William Penn's Holy Experiment in Education* (Philadelphia: Committee on Education, Philadelphia Yearly Meeting, 1992).

9. William Penn to Robert Turner, Anthony Sharp, and Roger Roberts, Westminster, April 12, 1681, in Soderlund, *William Penn*, 67.

10. William Penn to Robert Turner, August 25, 1681, Richard S. Dunn and Mary Maples Dunn, eds., *The Papers of William Penn* (Philadelphia: University of Pennsylvania Press, 1986), 2:110. See, particularly, Isa. 11, Dan. 2, and Rev. 3.

11. Penn wrote to Gulielma, his wife, advice in August 1682, including an admonition to guide their children into agricultural and domestic careers so they could

be "like Abraham and the holy ancients who pleased God and obtained a good report." In Soderlund, *William Penn*, 166.

12. William Penn to Thomas Janney, August 21, 1681, Dunn, et al., *Papers of William Penn*, 2:106.

13. Frost made this observation in his September 25, 1998, presentation at Pennsbury Manor " 'Wear the Sword.' " See Rev. 3:7–12.

14. Dunn, *Papers of William Penn*, 2:591.

15. William Penn to My Friends (Lenni Lenape Indians), October 18, 1681, in Soderlund, *William Penn*, 88.

16. William Penn to William Markham, April 10, 1681, in Dunn, *Papers of William Penn*, 2:85–86.

17. Donna Bingham Munger, *Pennsylvania Land Records* (Wilmington, Del.: Scholarly Resources, 1991), 27–28.

18. Dunn, *Papers of William Penn* 2:85–86.

19. The best description of the Land Office remains Lewis Evans, "A Brief Account of Pennsylvania, 1753," in Lawrence Henry Gipson, *Lewis Evans* (Philadelphia: Historical Society of Pennsylvania, 1939), 135–36.

20. Munger, *Pennsylvania Land Records*, 27–31.

21. Soderlund, *William Penn*, 155–57.

22. Ibid., 157–58.

23. Ibid., 160; Dunn, *Papers of William Penn*, 2:264–65.

24. Soderlund, *William Penn*, 84.

25. Ibid., 155.

26. Burdened by the costs of setting up a government, improving roads, and otherwise establishing his colony, Penn complained, in 1701 that Pennsylvania "Cost mee 10500 in the First 2: yrs." Penn to Charlwood Lawton, July 2, 1701, quoted in Richard Dunn and Mary Maples Dunn, eds., *The World of William Penn* (Philadelphia: University of Pennsylvania Press, 1986), 49. Still the Quaker proprietor preferred to remove Delaware encumbrance by purchase rather than force. He was not known to have complained about Delawares' pressing their advantage in land dealings.

27. Seed, *Ceremonies of Possession*, 24.

28. Lewis Evans, *Analysis of a General Map of the Middle British Colonies in America* (Philadelphia: B. Franklin, 1755), 11, in Gipson, *Lewis Evans*, 155.

29. Soderlund, *William Penn*, 156–58; Dunn, *Papers of William Penn*, 2: 262.

30. Soderlund, *William Penn*, 155–57.

31. Seed, *Ceremonies of Possession*, 1–40.

32. Soderlund, *William Penn*, 160.

33. Ibid., 84.

34. James H. Merrell, *Into the American Woods: Negotiators on the Pennsylvania Frontier* (New York: Norton, 1999), 27.

35. William Penn, "Some Account of the Province of Pennsylvania," in Soderlund, *William Penn*, 63.

36. Thomas Holme to William Penn, February 8, 1684/85, Etting Collection, Pemberton Papers, 28:7, Historical Society of Pennsylvania.

37. *Minutes and Proceedings of the Provincial Council of Pennsylvania* (Philadelphia: Jo. Severns, 1851–52), 31, May 28, 1692. William Penn to Thomas Holme, August 8, 1685. Both documents housed at the Historical Society of Pennsylvania.

38. Extract from Mr. Markham's Letter No. 1, dated August 22, 1686, Board of Trade Papers, Proprieties, 21:1, Historical Society of Pennsylvania; Penn Papers, Indian Affairs, Historical Society of Pennsylvania.

39. James O'Neil Spady, "Friendly Meetings: The Colonization of the Lenapes and the Discursive Antecedents of Penn's Treaty with the Indians," in Richter and Pencak, *Friends and Enemies*, 20.

40. Board of Trade Papers, Proprieties, 21:1, minutes of August 26, 1737, Historical Society of Pennsylvania.

41. Richard S. Dunn, "Pennywise and Pound Foolish," in Dunn and Dunn, *World of William Penn*, 51.

42. Ibid., 48–50; Soderlund, *William Penn*, 172.

43. Seed, *Ceremonies of Possession*, 25–31.

44. William Penn to John Blakling, November 29, 1683, Friends Library, London, quoted in Melvin B. Endy, *William Penn and Early Quakerism* (Princeton, N.J.: Princeton University Press, 1973), 355.

45. Soderlund, *William Penn*, 188.

46. Myers, *Narratives of Early Pennsylvania*, 233.

47. Soderlund, *William Penn*, 308–24.

48. Ibid.

49. Quoted in Frederick B. Tolles and E. Gordon Alderfer, eds., *The Witness of William Penn* (New York: Macmillan, 1957), 96.

50. Edward Morris to Roberts Vaux, January 24, 1827, Historical Society of Pennsylvania.

51. Penn Manuscripts, Indian Affairs, Indian Walk, 4:61, Historical Society of Pennsylvania.

52. Acount of the Walking Purchase by Moses Tetamie, Friendly Association Papers, 1:407, Quaker Collection, Haverford College.

53. Thomas Penn to Richard Peters, April 12, 1759, Supplementary Saunders Coates, 17:137, Historical Society of Pennsylvania.

54. Acount of the Walking Purchase by Moses Tetamie, 1:407.

55. Moses Tatamie's Account of Indian Claims, Taken from his Mouth at Easton, 1757, Pemberton Family Papers, Etting Collection, Historical Society of Pennsylvania.

56. Even Francis Jennings, in his 1966 dissertation, accepted the idea that a 1686 purchase had been consummated, though his later article on the documents of the Walking Purchase reconsiders that idea. Jennings, "Miquon's Passing," 315, and "Scandalous Indian Policy of William Penn's Sons;" Deeds and Documents of the Walking Purchase," *Pennsylvania History* 37, no. 1 (January 1970): 19–39.

57. Thomas Holme to William Penn, August 25, 1686, Etting Collection, Pemberton *Family Papers,* Historical Society of Pennsylvania.

58. Ibid.

59. Board of Trade Papers, Proprieties, 21:1, Historical Society of Pennsylvania. Penn Mss. Indian Affairs, Document C, Historical Society of Pennsylvania.

60. Acount of the "Walking Purchase" by Moses Tetamie, 1:407. This interpretation explains why there was a 1686 document, but also why it had conspicuous blanks; why the proprietary agents used it as their authoritative evidence of a purchase, but only after exhausting other possibilities; and finally why the Delawares did not remember any binding agreement reached in 1686. For evidence of Dela-

wares' willingness to relinquish rights to land south of Tohickon Creek based on the 1686 transaction, see Board of Trade Papers, Proprieties, 21:1, minutes of August 26, 1737, Historical Society of Pennsylvania.

61. Catherine Owens Peare, *William Penn: A Biography* (Philadelphia: J. B. Lippincott, 1957), 367.

62. Edward Armstrong, ed., *Correspondence Between William Penn and James Logan*, 2 vols. (Philadelphia: Historical Society of Pennsylvania, 1870–72), 1:48.

63. Thomas, John, and Richard Penn commissioned Richard Peters secretary of the Land Office October 26, 1737, and provincial secretary February 14, 1742/43, *Pennsylvania Archives* (Philadelphia: Jo. Sevens, 1852), 1:1:545.

64. Frederick B. Tolles, *James Logan and the Culture of Provincial America* (Boston: Little, Brown, 1957).

65. William Penn to James Logan, September 6, 1700, James Logan Papers, 1:15, Historical Society of Pennsylvania.

66. Munger, *Pennsylvania Land Records*, 29.

67. Charles Thomson, *An Enquiry into the Causes of the Alienation of the Delaware and Shawanese from the British Interest* (London: J. Wilkie, 1759), 67.

68. Deed marked by Sassoonan, et al, September 17, 1718, Friendly Association Papers, 1:15, Quaker Collection, Haverford College.

69. James Logan to John, Thomas, and Richard Penn, December 6, 1727, Historical Society of Pennsylvania; William J. Buck, *History of the Indian Walk* (Philadelphia: Edward S. Stuart, 1886), 41.

70. Ibid., 38.

71. Peare, *William Penn*, 402.

72. William Penn to Gulielma Penn, August 4, 1682, in Soderlund, *William Penn*, 165; Dunn, *Papers of William Penn*, 2:270; Dunn, "Pennywise and Pound Foolish," 51.

73. Quoted in Peare, *William Penn*, 394, 399.

74. Dunn, "Pennywise and Pound Foolish," 51.

75. Ibid., 41.

76. William Penn to Robert Turner, August 25, 1681, Dunn, *Papers of William Penn*, 2:110.

CHAPTER 5. WHAT YE INDIANS CALL YE HURRY WALK

The quotes opening the chapter are found in Soderlund, *William Penn*, 316, and account of the Walking Purchase by Moses Tetamie, Friendly Association Papers, 1:407.

1. Mark Monmonier, *Drawing the Line* (New York: Henry Holt, 1995), 105–6.

2. Jean R. Soderlund, "African Americans and Native Americans in John Woolman's World," unpublished manuscript, 11–12; "Crosswicks/ Crossweeksung," unpublished manuscripts in author's possession used by permission.

3. Neal Salisbury, "Native People and European Settlers in Eastern North America, 1600–1783," in *The Cambridge History of the Native Peoples of the Americas*, ed. Bruce G. Trigger and Wilcomb E. Washburn (Cambridge: Cambridge University Press, 1996), 1:436.

4. Account of the Walking Purchase by Moses Tetamie, 1:407.

5. William J. Heller *History of Northampton County, Pennsylvania and the Grand Valley of the Lehigh* (New York: American Historical Society, 1920), 49. Emphasis added.

6. A. B. Burrell, *Reminiscences of George La Bar* (Philadelphia: Claxton, 1870), 22.

7. John Penn and Richard Penn to Thomas Penn, May 12, 1734, Penn Letter Books 1:118–21, Historical Society of Pennsylvania.

8. Ibid..

9. Jennings, "Scandalous Indian Policy of William Penn's Sons," 19–39.

10. Frederick B. Tolles, *James Logan and the Culture of Provincial America.* "Letter from James Logan to the Society of Friends on Their Opposition in the Legislature to the Defence of the Colony," *Collections of the Historical Society of Pennsylvania* 1, no. 1 (May 1851): 34–35.

11. Quoted in Buck, *History of the Indian Walk*, 37–38.

12. James Logan to John, Thomas, and Richard Penn, December 6, 1727, James Logan Papers, Historical Society of Pennsylvania.

13. Account of the Walking Purchase by Moses Tetamie, 1:407.

14. Ibid.

15. Logan to John Chapman, March 12, 1730, Logan Letter Books, James Logan Papers, 3:141, Historical Society of Pennsylvania.

16. Logan to John Penn, December 6, 1727, Logan Correspondence, James Logan Papers, 1:89, Historical Society of Pennsylvania.

17. Logan to William Penn, December 6, 1727, Logan Letter Book 1717–1731, James Logan Papers, 515, Historical Society of Pennsylvania.

18. Logan to John Chapman, March 12, 1730. Logan Letter Book 3:129, James Logan Papers, Historical Society of Pennsylvania.

19. Logan to John, Thomas, and Richard Penn, July 29, 1728, James Logan Papers 10:45, Historical Society of Pennsylvania.

20. Letters of the Penn Family to James Logan, 2: 77, Penn Papers, Official Correspondence, Historical Society of Pennsylvania.

21. John Penn and Richard Penn to Thomas Penn, May 12, 1734, Penn Letter Books, 1: 118–21, Historical Society of Pennsylvania.

22. John Penn to Thomas Penn, undated, Penn Letter Books, 1:123, Historical Society of Pennsylvania.

23. Scheme of a Lottery for One Hundred Thousand Acres of Land in the Province of Pennsylvania, Friendly Association Papers, Quaker Collection, Haverford College; also in Munger, *Pennsylvania Land Records*, 72.

24. John Penn to Thomas Penn, Penn Letter Books, 1:123, Historical Society of Pennsylvania. *Statutes of Pennsylvania* 4:141–47.

25. Jennings, "Scandalous Indian Policy of William Penn's Sons," 23.

26. Logan to Penns, October 8, 1734, in *Pennsylvania Archives* (Philadelphia: Joseph Severns, 1852), 2:8:171–72.

27. Statement of Nutimus and other Delaware leaders to Jeremiah Langhorne, Bucks County Justice of the Peace, at Springfield, November 21, 1740, Penn Papers Indian Affairs, vol. 4, Indian Walk.

28. George Thomas to Delaware Indians, March 21, 1741, Penn Papers, Indian Affairs, vol. 4.

29. James Steel to Barefoot Brunson, April 12, 1735, James Steel Letterbook 1730–1741, Historical Society of Pennsylvania.

30. Thomas Penn to Richard Peters, July 17, 1752, Historical Society of Pennsyl-

vania. The Penns reserved this area, which became Easton, for themselves once they gained control of the Lehigh Valley.

31. James Steel to Timothy Smith, April 25, 1735, James Steel Letterbook 1730–1741, Historical Society of Pennsylvania.

32. James Steel to Timothy Smith and John Chapman, April 29, 1735, ibid.

33. Documents relating to the Trial Walk are in Manuscripts Collection folder 950, Friendly Association Papers, Quaker Collection, Haverford College.

34. The words and emphasis belong to Francis Jennings, "Scandalous Indian Policy of William Penn's Sons," 30. The 1686 document is most readily available in James Sullivan, ed., *The Papers of Sir William Johnson* (Albany: University of the State of New York in association with New York Division of Archives and History, 1921–65), 3:840.

35. Board of Trade Papers, Proprieties, 21:1. Penn Papers, Indian affairs, Document G.

36. Penn Papers, Indian Affairs, 3:100, Document G.

37. Ibid.

38. Account of the Walking Purchase by Moses Tetamie, 1:407.

39. Weshayanickon's Account of the Walking Purchase of 1686, Penn Papers, Indian Affairs, 4:61. Account of the Walking Purchase by Moses Tetamie, 1:407.

40. Acount of the Walking Purchase by Moses Tetamie, 1:407.

41. Ibid.

42. Ibid.

43. Sullivan, *The Papers of Sir William Johnson,* 3:767.

44. Logan to Weiser, October 18, 1736, James Logan Papers, 10:64. John Penn to James Logan, February 17, 1736/37, Penn Letter Books, 1:189; John Penn to Thomas Penn, ibid., 1:185.

45. Acount of the Walking Purchase by Moses Tetamie, 1:407. Penn Papers, Indian Affairs, 1:300, Document G.

46. Munger, *Pennsylvania Land Records,* 70.

47. Indenture, Recorded May 15, 1848, Bucks County Deed Books, book VII, p. 408–11, Bucks County Courthouse, Doylestown, Pa.

48. Clement Plumsted to John Penn, October 4, 1736, Penn Papers, Official Correspondence, 3:25.

49. On the lottery see Jennings, "Scandalous Indian Policy of William Penn's Sons," 33–34; Munger, *Pennsylvania Land Records,* 71–73.

50. William Parsons Papers, Field Notes, Historical Society of Pennsylvania.

51. Julian Boyd interpreted this missive as written by Iroquois and therefore missed James Logan's duplicity in the Walking Purchase and its aftermath. Julian Boyd, "Indian Affairs in Pennsylvania, 1736–1762," *Indian Treaties Printed by Benjamin Franklin* (Philadelphia: Historical Society of Pennsylvania, 1938), 27.

52. Logan to Weiser, October 1736, James Logan Papers, 11:26.

53. Ibid.

54. Logan to Weiser, October 18, 1736, James Logan Papers, 10:64.

55. Ibid.

56. Ibid.

57. Conrad Weiser to James Logan, October 27, 1736, James Logan Papers 10:65

58. Boyd, "Indian Affairs in Pennsylvania, 1736–1762."

59. *Internal Affairs Monthly Bulletin* 21, no. 1 (October 1953): 25.

60. Ibid., 25–26.

61. Weshaykanickon's Account of the Walking Purchase of 1686, Penn Papers, Indian Affairs, 4:61.

62. Board of Trade Papers, Proprieties, 21:1, minutes of August 26, 1737.

63. William Allen Deposition, Board of Trade Papers, Proprieties, 21:1.

64. Penn Manuscripts, 3:103, Historical Society of Pennsylvania.

65. William Allen Deposition, Historical Society of Pennsylvania.

66. Board of Trade Papers, Proprieties, 21:1, minutes of August 27, 1737.

67. Monmonier, *Drawing the Line*, 107.

68. Soderlund, *William Penn*, 160.

69. Board of Trade Papers, Proprieties, 21:1, minutes of August 26, 1737.

70. Penn Papers, Indian Affairs, 3:100, Document G.

71. Furniss, quoted in Ray Thompson's popularized, often unreliable *The Walking Purchase Hoax of 1737* (Fort Washington, Pa.: Bicentennial Press, 1973), 61.

72. "Philad: 4th 8th 1737 Recd. of James Steel Ten Pounds to be paid equally to James Yeats & Edward Marshall for walking the day & half on the Indian purchase in Bucks County also an English half Crown for E. Marshall for his good performance of the Journey." Penn Accounts, 1:38, Historical Society of Pennsylvania.

73. Some of the survey data were recorded in a field book kept by William Parsons: "7ber 22, 1737 from the Gap of Kittatinny on the West branch N 30 W about 7.1 miles to 5 Chestnut Oaks in a Circle one marked J PENN another T:P another RP 1737 thence N 56 E." On the following page, in older ink, is another survey, dated October 25, 1736, describing a tract of land for James Steel that lies inside the Walking Purchase. William Parsons Papers, Historical Society of Pennsylvania.

74. James Steel to Letitia Penn Aubrey, September 1737, in "Monroe, Pike, and Wayne Counties," unpublished MSS, Northampton County Papers, Historical Society of Pennsylvania.

75. Thomas Penn to John Penn and Richard Penn, October 11, 1737, Penn Papers, Official Correspondence, 3:55.

76. Rhode Island occupies 1,212 square miles.

77. Acount of the Walking Purchase by Moses Tetamie, Friendly Association Papers, 1:407.

CHAPTER 6. NO MORE BROTHERS AND FRIENDS

The quote opening the chapter is found in Delaware to Jeremiah Langhorne, Smithfield, January 3, 1741, Penn Manuscripts, Historical Society of Pennsylvania.

1. Moses Tatamy, Acount of Indian Complaints, Friendly Association Papers 1:65, Quaker Collection, Haverford College.

2. Charles Thomson, the Pennsylvania schoolmaster and later secretary of the Continental Congress, witnessed negotiations between Delawares and King George's representatives. He investigated the causes of Delaware alienation and published his findings in *An Enquiry into the Causes of the Alienation of the Delaware and Shawanese from the British Interest* (London: J. Wilkie, 1759). John Heckewelder, the Moravian missionary who learned Delaware ways firsthand and from his predecessor David Zeisberger, wrote *History, Manners, and Customs of the Indian Nations who once inhabited Pennsylvania* (Philadelphia: Historical Society of Pennsylvania,

1876). As Thomson did, Heckewelder documented Delaware dissatisfaction with the Walking Purchase. The later Moravian chronicler William Reichel relied on them.

3. Boyd, "Indian Affairs in Pennsylvania, 1736–1762," *Indian Treaties*, xxiii.

4. Heckewelder, *History*, 66–69.

5. Quoted in Buck, *History of the Indian Walk*, 37–38.

6. Andrew Trexler's Conversation with Indians About Walk, Friendly Association Papers 1:263.

7. Penn Manuscripts, Indian Affairs, 4:43.

8. William Parsons to Richard Peters, June 26, 1757, Richard Peters Papers, 4:94, Historical Society of Pennsylvania.

9. A. D. Chidsey, Jr., *A Frontier Village: Pre-Revolutionary Easton* (Easton, Pa.: Northampton County Historical and Genealogical Society, 1940), 16.

10. Jennings, "Miquon's Passing," 380–84. Also see Heller, *History of Northampton County*, 49.

11. Quoted in Buck, *History of the Indian Walk*, 37–38.

12. James Logan to John, Thomas, and Richard Penn, December 6, 1727, James Logan Papers, Historical Society of Pennsylvania.

13. Buck, *History of the Indian Walk*, 38.

14. Ibid., 43.

15. "Affair of Nicholas Depue," *[Pennsylvania] Department of Internal Affairs Monthly Bulletin* 21, no. 1 (October 1953): 32.

16. Buck, *History of the Indian Walk*, 205–6.

17. Wayland F. Dunaway, *The Scotch-Irish of Colonial Pennsylvania* (London: Archon Books, 1962), 54–55; William C. Reichel, *Memorials of the Moravian Church* (Philadelphia, 1870), 218.

18. Nazareth Diary, November 1, 1740, typescript, Moravian Historical Society, Nazareth, Pennsylvania. Vernon H. Nelson, trans., "Translation of Boehler's Account," *Transactions of the Moravian Historical Society* 27 (1992): 11–12. See also the Nazareth Diary entry for June 10/21, 1742. Pennsylvania Patent Books, F6, 102. Northampton County Deeds, C1, 156–64, Northampton County Courthouse, Easton, Pennsylvania, Buck, *History of the Indian Walk*, 45. "A History of the Beginnings of Moravian Work in America," *Publications of the Archives of the Moravian Church*, vol. 1 (Bethlehem, Pa.), 1955).

19. Nelson, "Translation of Boehler's Account," 15.

20. Elizabeth L. Myers, *The Upper Places: Nazareth, Gnadenthal, and Christian's Spring* (Easton, Pa.: Northampton County Historical and Genealogical Society, 1929), 4. W. N. Schwarze, "The Moravians in Northampton County," in Heller, *History of Northampton County*, 61–75.

21. See Nazareth Diary, March 11/22, 1742, and June 10/21, 1742, typescript, Moravian Historical Society, Nazareth, Pa.

22. Joseph M. Levering, *A History of Bethlehem, Pennsylvania, 1741–1892* (Bethlehem, Pa.: Times, 1903), 50–52, 153–56. Schwarze, "Moravians in Northampton County," in Heller, *History of Northampton County*, 61–75.

23. Quoted in Buck, *History of the Indian Walk*, 46.

24. Soderlund, *William Penn*, 160.

25. Anthony F. C. Wallace, *King of the Delawares, Teedyuscung, 1700–1763* (Syracuse, N.Y.: Syracuse University Press, 1990), 38.

26. Quoted in Jane T. Merritt, *At the Crossroads: Indians and Empires on a Mid-Atlantic Frontier, 1700–1763* (Chapel Hill: University of North Carolina Press, 2003), 96–97.

27. Nazareth Diary, July 3, 1742, typescript, Moravian Historical Society.

28. Ibid., December 26, 1742.

29. Thomas Penn to Richard Peters, July 17, 1752, Historical Society of Pennsylvania.

30. Ibid., April 12, 1759, Penn Manuscripts, Supplementary Saunders Coates, 17:92.

31. William Allen to John Penn, November 17, 1739, Penn Manuscripts, Official Correspondence, 3:91.

32. Delawares to Jeremiah Langhorne, Smithfield, January 3, 1741, Penn Manuscripts, Indian Affairs, vol. 4, Indian Walk, 30.

33. George Thomas to Delaware Indians, March 21, 1741, Penn Papers, Indian Affairs, vol. 4.

34. Francis Jennings, "Pennsylvania Indians," in *Beyond the Covenant Chain: The Iroquois and The Neighborhoods in Indian North America, 1600–1800,* ed. Daniel Richter and James Merrell, 90 (Syracuse, N.Y.: Syracuse University Press, 1987).

35. Sassoonan to Provincial Council, August 7, 1741, Records of the Provincial Council, Historical Society of Pennsylvania. Quote is in James Logan to the Proprietors, July 12, 1742, Richard Peters Papers, 1:89, Historical Society of Pennsylvania. *Minutes of the Provincial Council of Pennsylvania* (Harrisburg, Pa.: Theo. Fenn & Co.), 4:577–80.

36. *Minutes of the Provincial Council of Pennsylvania,* 4:578–580.

37. Ibid.

38. Jane T. Merritt, "Metaphor, Meaning, and Misunderstanding," in *Contact Points: American Frontiers from the Mohawk Valley to the Mississippi, 1750–1830,* ed. Andrew R. L. Cayton and Fredrika Teute (Chapel Hill: University of North Carolina Press, 1998), 81, emphasis added.

39. C. A. Weslager, "The Delaware Indians as Women," *Journal of the Washington Academy of Sciences* 34, no. 12 (1944): 381–88; C. A. Weslager, "Further Light on the Delaware Indians as Women," *Journal of the Washington Academy of Sciences* 37 (1947): 298–304; Jay Miller, "The Delaware as Women: A Symbolic Solution," *American Ethnologist* 1, no. 3 (1974): 507–14.

40. Ibid., 7:297.

41. *Minutes of the Provincial Council of Pennsylvania,* 2:546, 3:334.

42. For instance, Daniel Richter questioned Canassatego's meaning since Iroquoian scholarship emphasizes matrilineage, making Iroquois women landholders with many advantages not available to women in more patriarchal societies. Richter, "Natives, Refugees, and Walkers: The Peopling and Repeopling of the Lehigh Valley," paper given at the Bitting Conference: Historical Perspectives on the Lehigh Valley Region, Lehigh University, February 25, 2000. Jane Merritt made similar observations in "Metaphor, Meaning, and Misunderstanding," in Ceyton and Teute, *Contact Points,* 65–69, 77.

43. Archer Butler Hubert, ed., *David Zeisberger's History of the Northern American Indians* (Lewisburg, Pa.: Wennawoods, 1999), 34–35. Heckewelder, *History.*

44. *Minutes of the Provincial Council of Pennsylvania,* 2:546, 3:334. Jennings reiterates his case in "Brother Miquon: Good Lord!" in Dunn and Dunn, *World of William Penn,* 198.

45. Sassoonan, quoted in Minutes of Treaty of July 15, 1718, James Logan Papers, 11:7.

46. Jennings, "Pennsylvania Indians," in Richter and Merrell, *Beyond the Covenant Chain*, 80.

47. Sassoonan in Minutes of Treaty of July 15, 1718, James Logan Papers, 11:7.

48. Merritt, "Metaphor, Meaning, and Misunderstanding," 79.

49. William Penn observed firsthand that Delaware "Government is by Kings, which they call Sachema, and those by Succession, but always of the Mother's side; for Instance, the Children of him that is now King, will not succeed, but his Brother by the Mother, or the Children of his Sister, whose Sons (and after them the Children of her Daughters) will reign, for no Woman inherits; the Reason they render for this way of Descent, is, that their Issue may not be spurious." He noted, too, that Delaware "Wives are the true Servants of their Husbands: otherwise the Men are very affectionate to them." William Penn to the Committee of the Free Society of Traders, 1683, in Myers, *Narratives of Early Pennsylvania*, 231–35. Another early description corroborated Penn thus: Delaware "Government is Monarchial, and Successive, and ever of the Mothers (the surest) side, to prevent Spurious Issue. The Distaff (as in France) is excluded the Regal Inheritance." Gabriel Thomas, *An Historical and Geographical Account of the Province and Country of Pensilvania and of West-New-Jersey in America* (London, 1698), quoted in Sylvester Stevens, *The Keystone State* (New York: American Historical Company, 1956), 3.

50. Cynthia Eller, *The Myth of Matriarchal Prehistory* (Boston: Beacon Press, 2000), from an avowedly feminist perspective, challenges both the evidence for and the pragmatism of pervasive and deeply held myths of matriarchy in prehistoric cultures. Regula Trenkwalder Schonenberger, *Lenape Women, Matriliny, and the Colonial Encounter: Resistance and Erosion of Power* (c. 1600–1876) (New York: Peter Lang, 1991), a self-proclaimed "excursus in feminist anthropology," discredits itself with dogmatic theorization and numerous evidentiary errors.

51. Merritt, "Metaphor, Meaning, and Misunderstanding," 78.

52. Ibid.

53. Minutes of a Meeting in the Court House, Lancaster, Pennsylvania, May 13, 1757, in Boyd, *Indian Treaties*, 178.

54. Merritt, "Metaphor, Meaning, and Misunderstanding," 81.

55. Kathleen M. Brown, "The Anglo-Algonquian Gender Frontier," in *Negotiators of Change: Historical Perspectives on Native American Women*, ed. Nancy Schoemaker, 41 (New York: Routledge, 1995).

56. Richard Peters to Thomas Penn, August 25, 1742, Richard Peters Papers, Historical Society of Pennsylvania.

57. Acount of the Walking Purchase by Moses Tetamie, Friendly Association Papers 1:407.

CHAPTER 7. BORDER MEN, CIVILIZED INDIANS, AND SAVAGES

1. The quotes opening the chapter are found in A. B. Burrell, *Reminiscences of George La Bar* (Philadelphia: Claxton, 1870) and A. D. Chidsey Jr., *A Frontier Village:*

Pre-Revolutionary Easton (Easton, Pa.: Northampton County Historical and Genealogical Society, 1940), 18.

2. Reichel, *Memorials of the Moravian Church*, x.

3. Jane T. Merritt, *At the Crossroads: Indians and Empires on a Mid-Atlantic Frontier, 1700–1763* (Chapel Hill: University of North Carolina Press, 2003), 268.

4. Jane Merritt made this point in "Dreaming of the Savior's Blood," *William and Mary Quarterly*, 3rd ser. 54, no. 4 (October 1997): 723–46.

5. Sereno Edwards Dwight, ed., *Memoirs of the Reverend David Brainerd* (New Haven, Conn.: S. Converse, 1822), 176.

6. Ibid., 151, 168, 174–78.

7. James Steel to John Chapman, May 17, 1733, James Steel Letterbook, Historical Society of Pennsylvania.

8. "Count Zinzendorf and the Indians, 1742," in Reichel, *Memorials of the Moravian Church*, 26–27.

9. Pennsylvania Land Records, Applications, 1732–33:17; Patent Book A8:405–6; Patent Book A9:530–32, Pennsylvania State Archive, Harrisburg. The fullest treatment of Tatamy is William A. Hunter, "Moses (Tunda) Tatamy, Delaware Indian Diplomat," in Robert S. Grumet, ed., 258–73 *Northeastern Indian Lives 1632–1816* (Amherst: University of Massachusetts Press, 1996).

10. Zinzendorf, as quoted in Reichel, *Memorials of the Moravian Church*, 26–27.

11. *Pennsylvania Colonial Records* (Philadelphia: Joseph Severns, 1851–53), 4:624–25.

12. Richard Peters to Thomas Penn, November 21, 1742, Peters Letter Book V, Historical Society of Pennsylvania. Penn replied, "I hope the Governor has given such an answer to the Fork Indians as you say he intended, their assurance is indeed astonishing, you have not informed me how they [be]came converted to Calvinism and I suppose they are not acquainted with much of their doctrines." Thomas Penn to Richard Peters, Penn Letter Books, 2:25, Historical Society of Pennsylvania.

13. David Brainerd, *Mirabilia Dei Inter Indicos* (Philadelphia: William Bradford, 1746), 8.

14. Ibid.

15. Ibid., 9.

16. Dwight, *Memoirs*, 178.

17. Brainerd, *Mirabilia*, 9–10, emphasis in original.

18. Ibid., 11–12.

19. Ibid., 10–14.

20. He was so designated by the 1738 patent that granted him full rights to his farm. Pennsylvania Land Records, Patent Book, A8:405–06, Pennsylvania State Archives, Harrisburg.

21. Tatamy quoted in Hunter, "Moses (Tunda) Tatamy: Delaware Indian Diplomat," in Grumet, *Northeastern Indian Lives*, 264.

22. Bernhard Adam Grube, Diarium von Meniowolagamekah, May 14, 17, June 14, 1752, *Publications of the Archives of the Moravian Church* (Bethlehem, Pa., 1955). Minutes of the Provincial Council of Pennsylvania, *Pennsylvania Colonial Records* (Philadelphia: Joseph Severns, 1851–53), 8:463–72. *Pennsylvania Archives*, 3:707–9. Samuel Parrish, *Some Chapters in the History of the Friendly Association* (Philadelphia: Friends Historical Association, 1877), 117.

23. Pennsylvania Land Records, Applications 1732–1733:17, Pennsylvania State Archives, Harrisburg.

24. Quoted in Merritt, "Dreaming of the Savior's Blood," 730.

25. Quoted in Reichel, *Memorials of the Moravian Church*, 119–20.

26. Merritt, "Dreaming of the Savior's Blood," 731.

27. Wallaces interprets Teedyuscung's motivations in *King of the Delawares: Teedyuscung, 1700–1763* (Syracuse, N.Y.: Syracuse University Press, 1990), 37–44.

28. Reichel, *Memorials of the Moravian Church*, 220.

29. Ibid.

30. Quoted in Merritt, "Dreaming of the Savior's Blood," 731.

31. Reichel, *Memorials of the Moravian Church*, 196.

32. Moses Tatamy, Account of Indian Complaints, Friendly Association Papers, 1:65

33. Ibid.

34. Chidsey, *Frontier Village*, 23.

35. Reichel, *Memorials of the Moravian Church*, 192.

36. Ibid., 193–94. Albert F. Jordan, ed., "The Moravians and the Indians during the French and Indian War," *Transactions of the Moravian Historical Society* 22, no. 1 (1969): 2–11.

37. Peters to Thomas Penn, August 4, 1756 Letter Book, 1755–1757, Peters Papers.

38. Ibid.

39. Reichel, *Memorials of the Moravian Church*, 200; Buck, *History of the Indian Walk*, 222–23.

40. Spangenburg to Moravians, December 23, 1755, Bethlehem, quoted in Reichel, *Memorials of the Moravian Church*, 206.

41. Quoted in ibid., 207.

42. Reichel, *Memorials of the Moravian Church*, 207.

43. Heller, *History of Northampton County*, 78–79.

44. Jordan, "Moravians and the Indians during the French and Indian War," 5.

45. Robert Hunter Morris to Moravian Indians, December 4, 1755, Reichel *Memorials*, 211.

46. Reichel, 198–99, 221, 227.

47. Matthew Schropp to Governor William Denny, Bethlehem, April 20, 1757, in ibid., 213.

48. Reichel, *Memorials of the Moravian Church*, 217.

49. Buck, *History of the Indian Walk*, 222–29.

50. Petition from residents of Lower Smithfield, Northampton County, to James Hamilton, Lieutenant Governor and Commander-in-Chief of the Province of Pennsylvania, September 1, 1763, Historical Society of Pennsylvania.

51. Reichel, *Memorials of the Moravian Church*, 221.

52. Buck, *History of the Indian Walk*, 236–38.

53. Burrell, *Reminiscences of George La Bar*, 38–39.

54. Edward Shippen to William Allen, December 16, 1755, Historical Society of Pennsylvania.

55. Richard Peters to Thomas Penn, January 4, 1757, Richard Peters Pages.

56. Ibid., January 7, 1757.

57. Conrad Weiser to Thomas Penn, February 28, 1757, Historical Society of Pennsylvania.

58. Friendly Association Papers, 1:63. Quaker Collection, Haverford College.

59. Quoted in A. D. Chidsey Jr., *A Frontier Village: Pre-Revolutionary Easton* (Easton, Pa.: Northampton County Historical and Genealogical Society, 1940), 97.

60. *Pennsylvania Colonial Records*, 7:109.

61. Thomas Penn to William Peters, July 7, 1756, Historical Society of Pennsylvania.

62. Chidsey, *Frontier Village*, 21–22.

63. Merritt, "Metaphor, Meaning, and Misunderstanding," *Crossroads*, 268.

CHAPTER 8. APPEARING FAIR AND JUST

Quotes at the beginning of this chapter are from Soderlund, *William Penn*, 169, and Penn Manuscripts, Indian Affairs 3:20, Historical Society of Pennsylvania.

1. Moses Tetamie, Acount of Indian Complaints, Friendly Association Papers 1:65.

2. Thomson, *Enquiry into the Causes of the Alienation*. Frederick B. Tolles, "The Twilight of the Holy Experiment," *Bulletin of the Friends Historical Association* 45, no. 1 (Spring 1956): 30–37.

3. Tetamie, Acount of Indian Complaints, 1:65.

4. Minutes of the Friendly Association, April 14, 1756, Friendly Association Papers. Historical Society of Pennsylvania.

5. Theodore Thayer, "The Friendly Association," *Pennsylvania Magazine of History and Biography* 67, no. 4 (October 1943): 362.

6. Robert Diautolo, Jr., "The Early Quaker Perception of the Indian," *Quaker History* 72, no. 2 (1983): 110–11.

7. 175n19

8. Boyd, *Indian Treaties*, 153.

9. Samuel Parrish, *Some Chapters in the History of the Friendly Association* (Philadelphia: Friends Historical Association, 1877), 32, 37.

10. Boyd, *Indian Treaties*, 154–55; Parrish, *Some Chapters*, 33.

11. Ibid., *Indian Treaties*, 156.

12. Penn Papers, Indian Affairs, 3:20.

13. Ibid.

14. Ibid.

15. Ibid.

16. Boyd, *Indian Treaties*, 158.

17. Parrish, *Some Chapters*, 36.

18. Boyd, *Indian Treaties*, 166. Richard Peters to Thomas Penn, November 22, 1756, Richard Peters Papers, Letter Book, 1755–57, Historical Society of Pennsylvania. The mild version of the treaty minutes has contributed to the view that the Walking Purchase was less significant than Delawares contended. See, for instance, Julian Boyd, "Indian Affairs in Pennsylvania, 1736–1762," in Boyd, *Indian Treaties*, xxvii.

19. Friendly Association minutes, January 8, 1757, Friendly Association Papers; Historical Society of Pennsylvania; hereafter cited as Minutes.

20. Minutes, November 20, 1756.

21. Richard Peters to Thomas Penn, November 22, 1756, Richard Peters Papers, Letter Book, 1755–57. Historical Society of Pennsylvania.

22. Richard Peters Papers Letter Book, 147–48, Historical Society of Pennsylvania.

23. Thomas Penn to Richard Peters, March 12, 1757, Charles Roberts Collection, Quaker Collection, Haverford College.

24. Parrish, *Some Chapters*, 70.

25. Minutes, January 25, 1757.

26. Boyd., *Indian Treaties*, 197.

27. Ibid.

28. Ibid., 199.

29. Ibid., 200–201.

30. Ibid., 205.

31. Ibid., 205.

32. Ibid., 207.

33. Parrish, *Some Chapters*, 78, says, "The Governor expressed himself as willing to grant this reasonable request, but privately agreed with Weiser and Croghan, not to present the papers most desired by the Chief." The treaty minutes say that Charles Thomson copied the deeds, and though they are often incredible, Thomson seems to bear them out on this point. See Thomson, *Enquiry Into the Causes*, 119.

34. Quoted in Thompson's popularized, often unreliable *Walking Purchase Hoax*, 88.

35. Thompson mistakenly cites this report as issued "at the end of 1758," in 84.

36. Penn Papers, Indian Affairs, 3:20.

37. Ibid.

38. Ibid.

39. Pennsylvania Commissioners to Teedyuscung, June 14, 1762, in Sullivan, *Papers of Sir William Johnson*, 3: 759–60.

40. Wallace, *King of the Delawares*, 245, emphasis in original.

41. Meeting at Easton with Delawares, in Sullivan, *Papers of Sir William Johnson*, 3:762.

42. Ibid.

43. Ibid., 3:768.

44. Ibid., 3:769.

45. Ibid.

46. Ibid., 3:771.

47. Wallace, *King of the Delawares*.

48. Sullivan, *Papers of Sir William Johnson*, 3:772–73.

49. Ibid.

50. Ibid.

51. Ibid., 3:776.

52. Ibid., 3:786.

53. Ibid., 3:776.

54. Ibid., 3:786.

55. Ibid., 3:847.

56. Ibid.

57. Teedyuscung's speech to Sir William Johnson, Easton, Pennsylvania, June 24, 1762, Small Collection 043, Friends Historical Library, Swarthmore College. Also in Penn Papers, Indian Affairs, vol. 3.

58. Isaac Still, affidavit, June 23, 1762, Small Collection 043 *FHL, Swarthmore.*

59. Boyd, "Indian Affairs," in Boyd, *Indian Treaties.* Jennings, *Empire of Fortune,* 436–37, revises Boyd but sets these events in a different light.

60. Wallace, *King of the Delawares,* 248, says, "Israel Pemberton, seeing that his front man was being treated lightly, decided that now was the time to throw off all disguises. No longer was it Indian against Englishman. The quarrel stood in its true colors: Quaker against proprietor."

61. Ralph L. Ketchum, "Conscience, War, and Politics in Pennsylvania, 1755–1757," *William and Mary Quarterly* 3rd ser. 20, no. 3 (July 1963): 436.

62. Sir William Johnson to the Lords of Trade, August 1, 1762, Sullivan, *Papers of Sir William Johnson,* 3:850.

CHAPTER 9. DIMENSIONS OF DELAWARE POWER IN PENN'S WOODS

The quote opening the chapter is found in Boyd, *Indian Treaties,* 207.

1. An observer noted that Penn "is iconocized not for his Quakerism, or even for his founding of Pennsylvania, but rather for the manner in which these two issues converged in his dealings with Indians." Tuomi J. Forrest, "William Penn: Visionary Proprietor," http://xroads.virginia.edu.

2. James Merrell, *Into the American Woods: Negotiature on the Pennsylvania Frontier* (New York: Norton, 1999), 30.

3. Dunn, *Papers of William Penn,* 2:33–34. Alden T. Vaughan, *New England Frontier: Puritans and Indians 1620–1675* (Boston: Little, Brown, 1965).

4. J. William Frost, "Secularization in Colonial Pennsylvania," in *Seeking the Light,* edited by J. William Frost and John M. Moore, 105–27 (Wallingford, Pa.: Pendle Hill Publications, 1986).

5. Thomas F. Gordon, *The History of Pennsylvania, from Its Discovery by Europeans to the Declaration of Independence in 1776* (Philadelphia, 1829), 54.

6. Tolles, "Twilight of the Holy Experiment," 33–34.

7. William Penn to My Friends (Lenni Lenape Indians), October 18, 1681, in Soderlund, *William Penn,* 88.

8. Soderlund, *William Penn,* 155–57.

9. Minutes and Proceedings of the Provincial Council, May 28, 1692. William Penn to Thomas Holme, August 8, 1685. Both documents housed at the Historical Society of Pennsylvania.

10. Merrell, *American Woods,* 111.

11. Ibid., 129.

12. Fred Anderson, *Crucible of War* (New York: Vintage, 2000), 94–107.

13. Quoted in Jennings, *Empire of Fortune,* 165.

14. Moses Tatamy, Account of Indian Complaints, 1:65.

15. Reichel, *Memorials of the Moravian Church,* 192.

16. Wallace, *King of the Delawares,* 242, 265.

17. Merrell, *American Woods,* 52.

18. Sullivan, *Papers of Sir William Johnson,* 3:772–73.

19. Ibid., 3:771.

20. Ibid.

21. Merritt, *Crossroads*, 280.

22. Kupperman, *Indians and English*, 212, emphasis added.

23. Resolution Requesting a Warrant for 200 Acres for Tatamy, an Indian, 1769, Pennsylvania Land Papers, Moore Collection, Historical Society of Pennsylvania.

24. Hunter, "Moses (Tunda) Tatamy, Delaware Indian Diplomat," 258–72.

25. Merrell, *American Woods*, 145; Marshall J. Becker, "The Boundary between the Lenape and Munsee: The Forks of the Delaware as a Buffer Zone," *Man in the Northeast* 26 (1983): 1–20.

26. *Minutes of the Provincial Council of Pennsylvania*, 10 vols. (Harrisburg: Theo. Fenn & Co., 1851–52), 9:42. Merritt, *Crossroads*, 273.

27. Wallace, *King of the Delawares*, 252–66. Merritt, *Crossroads*, 276–77.

28. Joseph J. Mickley, *Brief Account of the Murders by the Indians and the Cause Thereof in Northampton County, Pennsylvania* (Philadelphia: Thomas William Stuckey, 1875), 28–29.

29. Heckewelder, *History*, 334.

30. Quoted in Krista Camenzind, "The March toward the Paxton Boys: Violence, Patriarchy, and Race during the Seven Years War," in Richter and Pencak, *Friends and Enemies*, 201–20. Camenzind ably develops this theme throughout the chapter, with relevance to the Delawares displaced by the Walking Purchase.

31. Gabriel Thomas, "A Historical Description of the Province and Country of West New Jersey in America," in Myers, *Narratives of Early Pennsylvania*, 341.

32. Soderlund, *William Penn*, 160. Hinderaker, *Elusive Empires*, 101–10.

33. Kupperman, *Indians and English*, 174–240

34. Endy, *William Penn and Early Quakerism*, 348–77.

35. Ibid., 368–69.

36. Richard Peters to Thomas Penn, November 21, 1742, Richard Peters Pages, Letter Book V. Thomas Penn to Richard Peters, Penn Letter Books, 2:25, Historical Society of Pennsylvania.

37. Dunn, *Papers of William Penn*, 2:33–34.

38. Soderlund, *William Penn*, 307, 308–24.

39. Ibid.

40. William Penn to My Dear Wife and Children, August 4, 1682, ibid., 169.

Bibliography

Primary Sources

Manuscript Collections

Board of Trade Papers, Proprieties. Historical Society of Pennsylvania. Philadelphia, Pennsylvania.

Bucks County Deed Books, Bucks County Courthouse, Doylestown, Pennsylvania.

County Papers. Historical Society of Pennsylvania. Philadelphia, Pennsylvania.

Etting Collection, Historical Society of Pennsylvania. Philadelphia, Pennsylvania.

Friendly Association Papers, Quaker Collection. Haverford College.

James Logan Papers. Historical Society of Pennsylvania. Philadelphia, Pennsylvania.

James Steel Letterbook. Historical Society of Pennsylvania. Philadelphia, Pennsylvania.

Jonah Thompson Papers, Small Collections. Friends Historical Library, Swarthmore College.

Nazareth Diary. Moravian Historical Society, Nazareth, Pennsylvania.

Northampton County Deeds. Northampton County Courthouse, Easton, Pennsylvania. Microfilmed by the Genealogical Society of Utah.

Northampton County Papers. Historical Society of Pennsylvania. Philadelphia, Pennsylvania.

Northampton County Property Records. Northampton County Courthouse, Easton, Pennsylvania. Microfilmed by the Genealogical Society of Utah.

Pemberton Family Papers, Historical Society of Pennsylvania. Philadelphia, Pennsylvania.

Penn Letter Books, Historical Society of Pennsylvania, Philadelphia, Pennsylvania.

Penn Manuscripts, Historical Society of Pennsylvania. Philadelphia, Pennsylvania.

Penn Papers, Indian Affairs. Historical Society of Pennsylvania. Philadelphia, Pennsylvania.

Penn Papers, Official Correspondence. Historical Society of Pennsylvania. Philadelphia, Pennsylvania.

Pennsylvania Land Papers. Moore Collection. Historical Society of Pennsylvania. Philadelphia, Pennsylvania.

Pennsylvania Land Records. Pennsylvania State Archives. Harrisburg, Pennsylvania.

Richard Peters Papers. Historical Society of Pennsylvania. Philadelphia, Pennsylvania.

Small Collection 043, Friends Historical Library, Swarthmore College.

William Parsons Papers. Historical Society of Pennsylvania. Philadelphia, Pennsylvania.

Published Primary Sources

Bierhorst, John. *Mythology of the Lenape.* Tucson: University of Arizona Press, 1995.

Boyd, Julian, ed. *Indian Treaties Printed by Benjamin Franklin.* Philadelphia: Historical Society of Pennsylvania, 1938.

Brainerd, David. *Mirabilia Dei Inter Indicos.* Philadelphia: William Bradford, 1746.

Browne, William H., ed. *Proceedings and Acts of the General Assembly of Maryland,* volume 19 of the *Archives of Maryland* (Baltimore: Maryland Historical Society, 1899).

Chidsey, A. D., Jr. *Penn Patents in the Forks of the Delaware.* Easton, Pa.: Northampton County Historical and Genealogical Society, 1937.

Dunn, Richard S., and Mary Maples Dunn, ed. *The Papers of William Penn.* 5 vols. Philadelphia: University of Pennsylvania Press, 1981.

Dwight, Sereno Edwards, ed. *Memoirs of the Reverend David Brainerd.* New Haven, Conn.: S. Converse, 1822.

Gipson, Lawrence Henry. *Lewis Evans.* Philadelphia: Historical Society of Pennsylvania, 1939.

Hamilton, Kenneth G., trans. and eds. *The Bethlehem Diary.* 2 vol. Bethlehem, Pa.: Archives of the Moravian Church, 1971.

Hubert, Archer B., and William N. Schwarze, eds. "David Zeisberger's History of North American Indians." *Ohio Archealogical and Historical Quarterly* 19 (1910).

James, B. B., and J. Franklin Jameson, eds. *Journal of Jasper Danckaerts 1679–1680.* New York: Scribner's, 1913.

Johnson, Amandus, ed. and trans. *The Instruction for Johan Printz, Governor of New Sweden.* Philadelphia: Swedish Colonial Society, 1930.

Logan, James. "Letter from James Logan to the Society of Friends on Their Opposition in the Legislature to the Defence of the Colony". *Collections of the Historical Society of Pennsylvania,* no. 1 (May 1851): 34–35.

Minutes of the Provincial Council of Pennsylvania. Philadelphia: Joseph Severns, 1851–1852. 10 vols. Vols. 4–10 printed in Harrisburg by Theo. Fenn. & Co.

Myers, Albert Cook. *Narratives of Early Pennsylvania West New Jersey and Delaware, 1630–1707.* New York, Scribner's, 1912.

———. *William Penn: His Own Account of the Lenni Lenape or Delaware Indians, 1683.* Moylan, Pa.: A. C. Myers, 1937.

Nelson, Vernon H., trans. "Translation of Boehler's Account." *Transactions of the Moravian Historical Society* 27 (1992): 11–16.

Pennsylvania Archives. Philadelphia: Joseph Severns, 1852. A collection of documents supplementing the companion series known as *Pennsylvania Colonial Records,* which contains the minutes of the Provincial Council, of the Council of Safety, and of the Supreme Executive Council of Pennsylvania.

Pennsylvania Colonial Records. Philadelphia: Joseph Severns,1851–1853. Minutes of the Provincial Council of Pennsylvania, from the organization to the termination of the proprietary government, March 10, 1683–September 17, 1775.

Publications of the Archives of the Moravian Church. Bethlehem, Pennsylvania, 1955.

Reichel, William C., comp. *Memorials of the Moravian Church.* 3 vols. Philadelphia, 1870.

Schwarze, W. N., trans. *The Dansbury Diaries: Moravian Travel Diaries, 1748–1755.* Camden, Maine: Picton, 1994.

Soderlund, Jean R., ed. *William Penn and the Founding of Pennsylvania.* Philadelphia: University of Pennsylvania Press, 1983.

Sullivan, James, ed. *The Papers of Sir William Johnson.* 14 vols. Albany: University of the State of New York in association with New York Division of Archives and History, 1921–65.

Thomson, Charles. *An Enquiry into the Causes of the Alienation of the Delaware and Shawanese.* London: J. Wilkie, 1759.

Tolles, Frederick B., and E. Gordon Alderfer, eds. *The Witness of William Penn.* New York: Macmillan, 1957.

Van Laer, A. J., trans. and ed. *Documents Relating to New Netherland 1624–1626.* San Marino, Calif.: Huntington Library, 1924.

Secondary Sources

Anderson, Fred. *Crucible of War.* New York: Vintage, 2001.

Barnes, Carol. "Subsistence and Social Organization of the Delaware Indians: 1600 A.D." *Bulletin of the Philadelphia Anthropological Society* 20, no. 1 (1968): 15–29.

Becker, Marshall J. "The Boundary between the Lenape and Munsee: The Forks of the Delaware as a Buffer Zone." *Man in the Northeast* 26 (1983): 1–20.

———. "Lenape Archeology: Archeological and Ethnohistoric Consideration in Light of Recent Excavations." *Pennsylvania Archeologist* 50, no. 4 (1980): 19–30.

———. "Lenape Land Sales, Treaties, and Wampum Belts." *Pennsylvania Magazine of History and Biography* 108 (1984): 351–56.

———. "Lenape Population at the Time of European Contact: Estimating Native Numbers in the Lower Delaware Valley." *Proceedings of the American Philosophical Society* 133, no. 2 (1989): 112–22.

———. "The Swedes and Dutch in the Land of the Lenape." *Pennsylvania Heritage* 10, no. 1 (1984): 20–23.

Bragdon, Kathleen. *Native People of Southern New England 1500–1650.* Norman: University of Oklahoma Press, 1996.

Bronner, Edwin. *William Penn's Holy Experiment: The Founding of Pennsylvania, 1681–1701.* New York: Temple University Publications; distributed by Columbia University Press, 1962.

Brookes, George S. *Friend Anthony Benezet.* Philadelphia: University of Pennsylvania Press, 1937.

Buck, William J. *History of the Indian Walk.* Philadelphia: Edward S. Stuart, 1886.

Burrell, A. B. *Reminiscences of George La Bar.* Philadelphia: Claxton, 1870.

Cayton, Andrew R. L., and Fredrika Teute. *Contact Points: American Frontiers from the Mohawk Valley to the Mississippi, 1750–1830.* Chapel Hill: University of North Carolina Press, 1998.

Chidsey, A. D., Jr. *A Frontier Village: Pre-Revolutionary Easton.* Easton, Pa.: Northampton County Historical and Genealogical Society, 1940.

Clyde, John C. *Genealogies, Necrology and Reminiscences of the Irish Settlement.* Easton, Pa.: Frazier, 1879.

Comfort, William W. "William Penn's Religious Background." *Pennsylvania Magazine of History and Biography* 68, no. 4 (October 1944): 341–58.

Condit, Uzal W. *History of Easton, Pennsylvania from the Earliest Times to the Present, 1739–1885.* Easton, Pa., 1885.

Cummings, Hubertis. *Richard Peters: Provincial Secretary and Cleric, 1704–1766.* Philadelphia: University of Pennsylvania Press, 1944.

Custer, Jay F. *Prehistoric Cultures of Eastern Pennsylvania.* Harrisburg: Pennsylvania Historical and Museum Commission, 1996.

Cutcliffe, Stephen H. "Colonial Indian Policy as a Measure of Rising Imperialism: New York and Pennsylvania, 1700–1755." *Western Pennsylvania Historical Magazine* 64, no. 3 (1982): 237–68.

———. "Indians, Furs, and Empires: The Changing Policies of New York and Pennsylvania, 1674–1768." PhD diss., Lehigh University, 1976.

Diautolo, Robert, Jr. "The Early Quaker Perception of the Indian." *Quaker History* 72, no. 2 (1983): 103–19.

Dunaway, Wayland F. *The Scotch-Irish of Colonial Pennsylvania.* London: Archon Books, 1962.

Dunn, Richard S., and Mary Maples Dunn, eds. *The World of William Penn.* Philadelphia: University of Pennsylvania Press, 1986.

Eller, Cynthia. *The Myth of Matriarchal Prehistory.* Boston: Beacon Press, 2000.

Endy, William B., Jr. *William Penn and Early Quakerism.* Princeton, N.J.: Princeton University Press, 1973.

Fairbanks, Joseph H. "Richard Peters: Provincial Secretary of Pennsylvania." PhD diss., University of Arizona, 1972.

Frost, J. William. " 'Wear the Sword as Long as Thou Canst': William Penn in Myth and History." Presented to the McNeil Center for Early American Studies Seminar Series, Pennsbury Manor, September 25, 1998.

Frost, J. William, and John M. Moore, eds. *Seeking the Light.* Wallingford, Pa.: Pendle Hill, 1986.

Geiter, Mary K. "The Restoration Crisis and the Launching of Pennsylvania, 1679–1681." *English Historical Review,* 112 (1997): 300–318.

Goddard, Ives. "Delaware." In *Handbook of North American Indians,* Vol. 15, *Northeast.* Edited by Bruce G. Trigger. Washington, D.C.: Smithsonian Institution, 1978.

Gordon, Thomas F. *The History of Pennsylvania.* Philadelphia: Carey, Lea & Carey, 1829.

Gordos, Edward Andrew, Sr. "Indian Trade in Pennsylvania 1730–1763." MA thesis, Lehigh University, 1949.

Grumet, Robert Steven. *Northeastern Indian Lives 1632–1816.* Amherst: University of Massachusetts Press, 1996.

———. "We Are Not So Great Fools: Delawarean Socio–Political Life 1630–1758." PhD diss., Rutgers University, 1979.

Haefali, Evan. "The Creation of American Religious Pluralism: Churches, Colonialism, and Conquest in the Mid-Atlantic, 1628–1688. PhD diss., Princeton University, 2000.

Heckewelder, John. *History, Manners, and Customs of the Indian Nations Who Once Inhabited Pennsylvania.* Philadelphia: Historical Society of Pennsylvania, 1876.

Heller, William J. "Bucks County North of the Lehigh River." *Bucks County Historical Society Proceedings* 4 (October 1909): 41–50.

———. *History of Northampton County, Pennsylvania and the Grand Valley of the Lehigh.* 3 vols. New York: American Historical Society, 1920.

Henry, Matthew S. *History of the Lehigh Valley* (Easton, Pa.: 1860).

Hinderaker, Eric. *Elusive Empires: Constructing Colonialism in the Ohio Valley 1673–1800.* Cambridge: Cambridge University Press, 1997.

Hoffecker, Carol E., ed. *New Sweden in America.* Newark: University of Delaware Press, 1995.

Ingle, Larry H. *First among Friends: George Fox and The Creation of Quakerism.* New York: Oxford University Press, 1994.

Jennings, Francis. *The Ambiguous Iroquois Empire.* New York: Norton, 1984.

———. *Empire of Fortune: Crowns, Colonies and Tribes in the Seven Years War in America.* New York: Norton, 1988.

———. "Miquon's Passing." PhD diss., University of Pennsylvania, 1966.

———. "The Scandalous Indian Policy of William Penn's Sons: Deeds and Documents of the Walking Purchase." *Pennsylvania History* 37, no. 1 (January 1970): 19–39.

Jordan, Albert F. "The Moravians and the Indians during the French and Indian War." *Transactions of the Moravian Historical Society* 22, no. 1 (1969): 2–11.

Jordon, J. W. "Moravian Immigration to Pennsylvania 1734–1765." *Pennsylvania Magazine of History and Biography* 33 (1909): 228–48.

Keith, Charles P. *Chronicles of Pennsylvania from the English Revolution to the Peace of Aix-la-Chapelle, 1688–1748.* 2 vols. Philadelphia: 1917.

Ketchum, Ralph L. "Conscience, War, and Politics in Pennsylvania, 1755–1757." *William and Mary Quarterly* 3rd ser. 20 (1963): 416–39.

Kinsey, Fred, III. "Eastern Pennsylvania Prehistory: A Review." *Pennsylvania History* 50 (1983): 69–100.

Kraft, Herbert C., ed. *The Lenape: Archeology, History, and Ethnography.* Newark: New Jersey Historical Society, 1986.

———. *The Lenape Indian.* South Orange, N.J.: Archeological Research Center, Seton Hall University, 1984.

Kuehner, Arlyle Kathleen. "Pennsylvania under Lieutenant Governor William Denny, 1756–1759." MA thesis, Lehigh University, 1935.

Kupperman, Karen Ordahl. *Indians and English: Facing Off in Early America.* Ithaca, N.Y.: Cornell University Press, 2000.

Levering, Joseph M. *A History of Bethlehem, Pennsylvania, 1741–1892.* Bethlehem, Pa.: Times, 1903.

Lovejoy, David S. *Religious Enthusiasm in the New World.* Cambridge, Mass.: Harvard University Press, 1985.

MacLeod, William C. "Family Hunting Territory and Lenape Political Organization." *American Anthropologist* 24, no. 4 (1923): 448–63.

Marietta, Jack D. "Conscience, the Quaker Community, and the French and Indian War." *Pennsylvania Magazine of History and Biography* 95 (1971): 3–27.

Merrell, James. *Into the American Woods: Negotiators on the Pennsylvania Frontier.* New York: Norton, 1999.

Merritt, Jane T. *At the Crossroads: Indians and Empires on a Mid–Atlantic Frontier, 1700–1763.* Chapel Hill: University of North Carolina Press, 2003.

———. "Dreaming of the Savior's Blood: Moravians and the Indian Great Awakening in Pennsylvania." *William and Mary Quarterly,* 3rd ser. 54, no. 4 (October 1997): 723–46.

Mickley, Joseph J. *Brief Account of the Murders by the Indians and the Cause Thereof in Northampton County, Pennsylvania.* Philadelphia: Thomas William Stuckey, 1875.

Miller, Jay. "The Delaware Indians as Women: A Symbolic Solution." *American Ethnologist* 1, no. 3 (1974): 507–14.

Monmonier, Mark. *Drawing the Line.* New York: Henry Holt, 1995.

Morrill, John, Paul Slack, and Daniel Woolf, eds. *Public Duty and Private Conscience in Seventeenth Century England.* Oxford: Clarendon Press, 1993.

Moulton, Phillips S., ed. *The Journal and Major Essays of John Woolman.* Richmond, Ind.: Friends United Press, 1989.

Munger, Donna B. *Pennsylvania Land Records: A History and Guide for Research.* Wilmington, Del.: Scholarly Resources, 1991.

Myers, Elizabeth L. *The Upper Places: Nazareth, Gnadenthal, and Christian's Spring.* Easton, Pa.: Northampton County Historical and Genealogical Society, 1929.

Newcomb, William W., Jr. *The Culture and Acculturation of the Delaware Indians.* Ann Arbor: Museum of Anthropology, University of Michigan, 1956.

———. "The Walum Olum of the Delaware Indians in Perspective." *Texas Journal of Science* 7 (1955): 57–63.

Olmstead, Earl P. *David Zeisberger: A Life among the Indians.* Kent, Ohio: Kent State University Press, 1997.

Parrish, Samuel. *Some Chapters in the History of the Friendly Association.* Philadelphia: Friends Historical Association, 1877.

Pearce, Roy Harvey. *The Savages of America: A Study of the Indians and the Idea of Civilization.* Baltimore: Johns Hopkins University Press, 1953.

Peare, Catherine Owens. *William Penn: A Biography.* Philadelphia: Lippincott, 1957.

Pencak, William A., and Daniel K. Richter, eds. *Friends and Enemies in Penn's Woods: Indians, Colonists, and the Racial Construction of Pennsylvania.* State College: Penn State University Press, 2004.

Pietak, Lynn Marie. "Trading with Strangers: Delaware and Munsee Strategies for Integrating European Trade Goods, 1600–1800." PhD diss., University of Virginia, 1995.

Prentiss, Henry Moeller. "The Life of James Hamilton, Esquire, Lieutenant Governor of Pennsylvania." MA thesis, Lehigh University, 1930.

Raup, Hallock F. "Settlement and Settlement Forms of the Pennsylvania Dutch at the Forks of the Delaware, Northampton County, Pennsylvania." PhD diss., University of California, Berkeley, 1935.

Richards, Jay C. *Flames along the Delaware: The French and Indian War in the New Jersey Frontier and Northampton County, Pennsylvania.* Belvidere, N.J.: J. C. Richards, 1997.

Richter, Daniel K. "War and Culture: The Iroquois Experience." William & Mary Quarterly 40 (1983): 528–59.

———, and James H. Merrell, eds. *Beyond the Covenant Chain.* Syracuse, N.Y.: Syracuse University Press, 1987.

Rountree, Helen. *Eastern Shore Indians of Virginia and Maryland.* Charlottesville: University Press of Virginia. 1998.

———. *The Powhatan Indians of Virginia.* Norman: University of Oklahoma Press, 1989.

Schlenther, Stanley. "Training for Resistance: Charles Thomson and Indian Affairs in Pennsylvania." *Pennsylvania History* 50 (1983): 185–217.

Schonenberger, Regula Trenkwalder. *Lenape Women, Matriliny, and the Colonial Encounter: Resistance and Erosion of Power (c. 1600–1876).* New York: Peter Lang, 1991.

Seed, Patricia. *Ceremonies of Possession in Europe's Conquest of the New World 1492–1640.* Cambridge: Cambridge University Press, 1995.

Shoemaker, Nancy, ed. *Negotiators of Change: Historical Perspectives on Native American Women.* New York: Routledge, 1995.

Simms, Steven R. "Changing Patterns of Information and Material Flow at the Archaic Woodland Transition in the Northeastern United States." *Pennsylvania Archeologist* 49, no. 4 (1979): 30–44.

Soderlund, Jean R. "African Americans and Native Americans in John Woolman's World." Unpublished manuscript in author's possession.

———. "Crosswicks/Crossweeksung." Unpublished manuscript in author's possession.

Smaby, Beverly. *Transformation of Moravian Bethlehem.* Philadelphia: University of Pennsylvania Press, 1988.

Stevens, Sylvester. *The Keystone State.* New York: American Historical Company, 1956.

Sugrue, Thomas J. "The Peopling and Depeopling of Early Pennsylvania: Indians and Colonists, 1680–1720." *Pennsylvania Magazine of History and Biography* 106, no. 1 (January 1992): 3–31.

Thayer, Theodore. "The Friendly Association." *Pennsylvania Magazine of History and Biography* 67, no. 4 (October 1943): 357–76.

Thompson, Ray. *The Walking Purchase Hoax of 1737.* Fort Washington, Pa.: Bicentennial Press, 1973.

Tolles, Frederick B, ed. *Handbook of North American Indians.* Vol. 15. *Northeast.* Washington, D.C.: Smithsonian Institution, 1978.

———. *James Logan and the Culture of Provincial America.* Boston: Little, Brown, 1957.

———. "The Twilight of the Holy Experiment." *Bulletin of the Friends Historical Association* 45, no. 1 (Spring 1956): 30–37.

———, and Wilcomb E. Washburn, eds. *The Cambridge History of the Native Peoples of the Americas.* London: Cambridge University Press, 1996.

Tully, Alan. "Politics and Peace Testimony in Mid-Eighteenth Century Pennsylvania." *Canadian Review of American Studies* 13 (1982): 159–77.

Vaughan, Alden T. *New England Frontier: Puritans and Indians, 1620–1675.* Boston: Little, Brown, 1965.

Wallace, Anthony F. C. *King of the Delawares: Teedyuscung, 1700–1763.* Syracuse, N.Y.: Syracuse University Press, 1990.

———. "New Religious Beliefs among the Delaware Indians, 1600–1900." *Southwestern Journal of Anthropology* 12 (1956): 1–21.

———. "Political Organization and Land Tenure among Northeastern Indians." *Southwestern Journal of Anthropology* 13 (1957): 301–21.

———. "Women, Land, and Society: Three Aspects of Aboriginal Delaware Life." *Pennsylvania Archealogist* 17:1–4 (1947): 1–36.

Wallace, Paul A.W. *Indians in Pennsylvania.* Harrisburg: Pennsylvania Historical and Museum Commission, 1999.

Weslager, Charles A. *The Delaware Indians: A History.* New Brunswick, N.J.: Rutgers University Press, 1972.

———. "The Delaware Indians as Women." *Journal of the Washington Academy of Sciences* 34, no. 12 (1944): 381–88.

———. "Further Light on the Delaware Indians as Women." *Journal of the Washington Academy of Sciences* 38 (1947): 298–304.

White, Richard. *The Middle Ground: Indians, Empires, and Republics in the Great Lakes Region 1650–1815.* New York: Cambridge University Press, 1991.

Wilson, Muriel Louise. "Thomas Penn, Chief Proprietor of Pennsylvania: A Study of the Proprietorial Activities as Evidenced by the Penn Letter Books." MA thesis, Lehigh University, 1932.

Index